Braun
Large-scale Privatization via Auctions

GABLER EDITION WISSENSCHAFT

Kasseler Wirtschafts- und
Verwaltungswissenschaften; Band 7

Herausgegeben von Dr. Heinz Hübner, Dr. Jürgen
Reese, Dr. Peter Weise und Dr. Udo Winand,
Univ.-Professoren des Fachbereiches
Wirtschaftswissenschaften, Universität-Gh Kassel

Die Schriftenreihe dient der gebündelten Darstellung der vielfältigen
wissenschaftlichen Aktivitäten des Fachbereichs Wirtschaftswissenschaften der Universität-Gh Kassel. Er umfaßt die Fachgebiete
Betriebswirtschaftslehre, Volkswirtschaftslehre, Verwaltungswissen-
schaft und Wirtschaftsinformatik. Die Reihe ist jedoch auch offen für
die Veröffentlichung von Arbeiten aus „verwandten" Fachgebieten
und Ergebnissen aus interdisziplinären Projekten mit ausgeprägtem
Bezug zu ökonomischen Fragestellungen.

Jocelyn Braun

Large-scale Privatization via Auctions

The case of land
in transforming economies

With a foreword by
Prof. Dr. Rainer Stöttner

DeutscherUniversitätsVerlag

Die Deutsche Bibliothek - CIP-Einheitsaufnahme

Braun, Jocelyn:
Large-scale Privatization via Auctions : the case of land in transforming
economies /Jocelyn Braun. With a foreword by Rainer Stöttner.
- Wiesbaden : Dt. Univ.-Verl. ; Wiesbaden : Gabler, 1998
   (Kasseler Wirtschafts- und Verwaltungswissenschaften ; Bd. 7)
   (Gabler Edition Wissenschaft)
   Zugl.: Kassel, Univ., Diss., 1998
   ISBN 978-3-8244-6777-8   ISBN 978-3-322-97775-5 (eBook)
   DOI 10.1007/978-3-322-97775-5

Gabler Verlag, Deutscher Universitäts-Verlag, Wiesbaden
© Betriebswirtschaftlicher Verlag Dr. Th. Gabler GmbH, Wiesbaden, 1998
Der Deutsche Universitäts-Verlag und der Gabler Verlag sind Unternehmen der
Bertelsmann Fachinformation GmbH.

http://www. gabler-online.de

Höchste inhaltliche und technische Qualität unserer Produkte ist unser Ziel. Bei der Produktion und
Auslieferung unserer Bücher wollen wir die Umwelt schonen: Dieses Buch ist auf säurefreiem und
chlorfrei gebleichtem Papier gedruckt.

Die Wiedergabe von Gebrauchsnamen, Handelsnamen, Warenbezeichnungen usw. in diesem
Werk berechtigt auch ohne besondere Kennzeichnung nicht zu der Annahme, daß solche Namen
im Sinne der Warenzeichen- und Markenschutz-Gesetzgebung als frei zu betrachten wären
und daher von jedermann benutzt werden dürften.

Lektorat: Ute Wrasmann / Brigitte Knöringer

ISBN 978-3-8244-6777-8

Foreword

The collapse of socialist economies has demonstrated the superiority of market-driven economies historically. The market economy has by no means established itself as a reliable and never-erring problem-solving device in a broad social and economic context. However, "capitalism", as the market-driven economic system is sometimes called with an ideological twist, still lacks a clear-cut and unambiguous structure. Among others, there seems to be a clear evidence of market failures resulting from a variety of causes. For example, the market mechanism may be "blind" with respect to the social and environmental needs of the society, thus stifling social welfare in the long run. Moreover, private enterprise does not easily lend itself to the production of public goods because the lack of the exclusion principle invites free rider attitudes.

In 1989, formerly socialist economies, especially in Eastern Europe, suddenly lost their so far seemingly solid social, economic and judicial foundations; the "capitalist" system offering itself as the only alternative. Nobody could be really happy with the sudden upheaval that posed many questions and practically offered no answers. It was quite clear that market structures could not replace the former socialist structures within an eye's wink, and without any specific modifications. But which modifications would seem fit, taking into account the special circumstances of a country? How quickly should the transformation process be implemented? Was the "big bang" method or the gradual method to be preferred?

In the first case, there would be risks of jeopardizing the transformation, mainly by losing the support of the broad general public threatened by the collapse of familiar economic and social structures. In the second case, the co-existence of incompatible elements, namely the socialist and capitalist elements of social and economic organizations, would lead to losses in efficiency and in the emotional drive behind the transformation process.

The work presented here addresses one special aspect of the transformation problem, namely the privatization of agricultural land on the territory of the former socialist countries. The author provides a theoretical and empirical treatment of this special aspect by embedding it in the complex causal structures of transformation and privatization theory. She is able to identify auctions as the most efficient mechanism to implement large-scale privatization schemes. These, in turn, constitute an indispensable pre-condition of a successful transformation. Thus, focusing on the privatization of agricultural land does not restrict the generalization of the theoretical argument to all sorts of privatization projects.

The author has founded her reasoning on solid theoretical grounds. Mechanism design theory, as outlined by W. Vickrey in the early sixties and further developed by L. Hurwicz and R.B. Myerson, plays a central role in her theoretical argument. The plain and simple question in transforming economies just boils down to the following: How can a system of economic incentives be implemented in such a way that optimal decisions under uncertainty emerge? Ms. Braun finds that auctions provide a superior mechanism in setting off large-scale privatization projects.

In addition, Ms. Braun draws heavily upon the "neo-institutionalist" or principal agent theories provided by G. A. Akerlof, M.C. Jensen, W.H. Meckling, D.M. Jaffee, T. Russel, B.R. Holmström , O.E. Williamson and others. The author hereby is paying tribute to the fact that privatization measures pose a variety of typical principal-agent problems. The relationship between the state and the buyers, the principal being the state pursuing the privatization scheme and the agent being the potential buyer of assets that so far have been in public ownership, clearly stand in a principal agent environment: The principal tries to make sure that the agent will secure the utmost benefit for society by utilizing the privatized asset. The agent, however, may try and cheat the principal as to his true type; thus the principal's choice may lead to adverse selection problems. Moreover, the agent may do a lazy and dismal job yielding to the temptations of moral hazard after assigning the contract. The author successfully shows that the auction mechanism proves to be superior, because it urges the agent to reveal honestly his or her merits as well as his or her weaknesses.

The principal-agent problem is embedded in the broader theoretical context of asymmetric information. The author demonstrates that a large part of the transformation problem essentially consists of problems of asymmetric information. In case of privatization measures, the parties engaging on the scheme practically know very little of each other. The efficiency and smoothness of the transformation process will very much depend upon the degree of mitigating informational asymmetry. In the worst of all cases, contracting would not be possible because of the parties distrusting each other. The author once again demonstrates impressively that the best solution to the problem of asymmetric information lies on a fair and sufficiently transparent contractual mechanism. Once again, auctions are best suited to clear up the playing field of the contractual parties because they urge the bidder - - the agent - - to reveal his or her willingness to pay. In his/her own best interest, he/she will reveal his/her willingness to pay, otherwise risking not winning the auction. Signaling the highest willingness to pay is at least indicative of the ability of making the most productive use of the privatized asset. Putting the asset to its most productive use means maximizing social welfare. Thus, auctions seem to be the mechanism that guarantees welfare maximization.

Moreover, the author uses the game-theoretic approach in order to derive her conclusions. The government can be seen as a principal trying to engage others, the agents, via privatization, to do its job of social welfare maximization. Viewed from a game-theoretic perspective, the principal as well as the agent(s) want to emerge from the game as winners. The government wants to make sure that social welfare will be maximized; the private owner, on the other hand, wants to maximize his private utility. Existing informational deficits on both sides create the temptation of cheating for both parties. Anybody taking part in the game is aware of this. In order to minimize any potential loss in playing the game, each party is interested in reducing informational deficits. Each party will try to induce the counterparty to reveal its private knowledge, thereby also revealing the motives behind each party's actions. This, by the way, makes it perfectly clear that the information problem can only be solved by establishing a mechanism that leads to efficient contracting.

Finally, it should be stressed that the author develops her argument in fair distance to the neoclassical paradigm of market equilibrium, which is based on conditions of perfect information. Her analysis is strictly intertwined with the game-theoretic background, showing how an auction-based privatization should be modeled adequately by focusing on the strategic component of the mechanism. At the same time, the reasoning has to take proper account of the fact that privatization works under the conditions of imperfect information. For this reason, the author employs the equilibrium analysis of the Bayesian-Nash type.

Ms. Braun outlines her arguments and derives her results on a high level of strict economic reasoning. She provides a thorough and deep insight into the privatization problems to be encountered in all transforming economies. Thus, her work contributes to closing a gap in our current knowledge of transformation economics. At the same time, she takes an honest stand by making perfectly clear the limits of her approach. These refer especially to the fact that value judgements and personal biases of the bidder may not be modeled. For example, the possibility of a purely efficiency-oriented market economy leading to discrepancies between individual and social welfare cannot be dismissed in any way. But, as the author correctly stresses, we practically do not have any acceptable alternative. Discouraging private initiative and entrepreneurship by letting administrative regulations proliferate cannot be the answer of a market economy. If privatization leads to social and economic effects not generally accepted, the market mechanism will have to react and produce better solutions. Thus, the market economy proves to rest on a self-organizing process that has been time-tested.

The work of Ms. Braun takes the reader to the frontier of research in transformation and privatization economics. Based on a concise outline of the state of the art of all relevant fields of economic theory, she shows the way to as yet poorly investigated territory, and even beyond.

Rainer Stöttner

Preface

When I was searching for an appropriate research topic, the idea to take up something new and exciting brought me to game-theoretic models. At the time, my knowledge of auctions was limited to the institutions I have always seen selling artworks. In short, I have practically never heard of auction theory, till I started to search for literature on sell-off mechanisms.

Getting deeper into the topic of auctions and mechanism design was made easier by the scholarly environment I was lucky to be part of at the Chair of Prof. Dr. Wilhelm Brandes of the Institute of Agricultural Economics, University of Goettingen. With the help of colleagues, the topic has evolved into a research project on land privatization via auctioning, which was funded by the *Deutsche Forschungsgemeinschaft*. The *Workshop on Economic Theory* at the Institute has helped me focus my thinking regarding my analysis in many ways. From the initial emphasis on the land privatization problems in the former East Germany, the research has taken a holistic perspective by going beyond the borders to the ex-socialist countries of Eastern Europe. This has also helped the research considerably well since the sticky political economy issues that has bogged down the East German land privatization program has been contained into manageable levels in the analysis, allowing a greater focus on the relevance of the design process in privatizing highly political resources in light of economic transformation.

Having the research done at the University of Goettingen in conjunction with the close supervision of Prof. Dr. Rainer Stoettner at the Faculty of Economics and Business, University of Kassel has created an interesting perspective in the research as it appears now in this book. I am grateful for the opportunity to have had the regular discussions with Prof. Stoettner and his staff. These had been truly fruitful and encouraging in keeping on with the seemingly unending and sometimes frustrating task of writing.

As is always the case, there are many people to thank, but I feel that some very special ones need to be mentioned. At the University of Goettingen, I would like to express my gratitude to my colleagues and/or ex-colleagues Dr. Alfons Balmann, Prof. Dr. Tilman Becker, Thomas Berger, Dr. Hans-Joachim Budde, Ludger Hinners-Tobrägel, Dr. Heinrich Hockmann, Dr. Guido Recke, Dr. Hans-Peter Weikard, as well as Wolfgang Peinemann and Martina Reichmann.

At the University of Kassel, thanks are due to Sophie Robé, Karin Hoppstaedter, Jochen Dittmar, Norbert Mueller, and Barbara Jung, as well as the two other members of my Ph.D. defense panel, Prof. Dr. Peter Weise and PD Dr. Thomas Eger.

Last but not least is of course the gratitute to my family , Andreas, Margaux and - perhaps the greater achievement during the struggle towards the completion of the Ph.D.- Baby Benedict. *Die moralische Unterstützung ist gelungen!*

Jocelyn Braun

Table of Contents

List of Tables

List of Figures

1. Introduction: Overview of the problems and issues in transformation

The transition phenomenon involves not just a change in economic systems, but also a change in thinking. Our collective experience so far with the transition process is relatively limited (p. 7).

...notwithstanding these early lessons, we find ourselves at a steep end of the learning curve. There is much that we do not know about how to achieve a successful transition. (p. 8)

Lewis Preston in his keynote address
World Bank 1994 Annual Conference on
Development Economics in Washington DC

1.1 Macroeconomic level issues

The breakdown of the socialist governments of the Eastern and Central European countries has led to a series of events that prompted the gradual movement of these countries from a totalitarian to a democratic form of government. Parallel to this political/ideological change is the movement from centrally planned economies into market economies. The transformation of the economies was and still is a challenge that the policy-makers in these ex-socialist governments face. The main task of the new governments in these countries during the period of transition is to build and organize the institutions that are inherently seen (and required) in a functioning market economy. The task is huge, as it requires a macroeconomic structural change which involves all sectors of the economy.

The reform that the economies in transition have adopted could be classified into two types: a reform based on the *big bang* principle, and a *gradual reform* policy.[1] Poland and Russia adopted the big bang (or sometimes called shock treatment) policy. The reform involves undertaking activities all at the same time, in order to avoid the costs associated with the emergence of distortions if some sectors of the economy are not allowed to adjust to the changes. Such distortions could arise because the agents get the "false" messages within the economy and thus trade at the "wrong" prices, promoting a misallocation of resources, at least in the short run. In East Germany, the big bang was a necessary move since the reunification meant the adoption of the West

---

[1] See Siebert (1993) and Funke (1994) for further discussion.

German political, economic and social system by the eastern states. The gradual reform approach, on the other hand, has been a policy adopted by Hungary, and the focus of the reform is on some sectors viewed to be strategic; for instance, liberalization in the trade sector.

Although there is little evidence to support it, researchers in the field of transformation economics are now starting to think that the big bang principle could have an advantage over the gradual reform policy. This is because at the initial phase of the transition period, there is much euphoria in the air for the economic change that makes the institutional development towards the move to a market economy easier to implement. As economies move on, old structures become sticky and difficult to change. In addition, the economies are burdened with new problems that were not initially anticipated, and so their current efforts are also directed at solving these new problems. Politicians also learn quickly how to handle their economic management activities to their best interest, and thus there is an observed rise in corruption and bribery. To this date there is no consensus on what the right economic prescription might be for these countries in transition. Experience is still being collected in the course, and the end of the transition could not be defined.

In recollecting the past years since the change has started in 1989 marked by the fall of the Berlin Wall, it is not easy to draw up conclusions as to the general status of the transforming economies. Although some progress has been made in the course, many of the initial expectations that followed the euphoria have not been met. In the initial period, there was a widespread belief on the ability of the new capitalist system to ease the life of the people. As it turned out, the transition process has, in most economies, led to a long period of recession coupled with other economic and social problems, all of which were somehow overlooked in the initial planning process. Some of the transition economies have turned back to support the old communist parties, and social unrest has sometimes evolved out of the frustrations of the people. In the following sections, a brief review of the macroeconomic framework that surrounds the transition problem is presented.

1.1.1 Growth and Development

The transition process is an entirely new phenomenon, and the traditional economic development analysis does not provide direct answers to the many questions that arise

2

in the process of change experienced in the ex-socialist economies. The concept of economic transition is, till the end of the 1980s, unknown. Little knowledge has since then been gained, and ideas are still needed to promote its understanding. Although the problem of development in transition economies may be similar to the issues found in developing countries, there are fundamental differences. The preconditions are much too different to warrant a direct application of the experiences gained. As a result, many policies implemented could be considered as experimental, relying on pure logic, popular sentiments, and the strength of the recommendations of the consultants to the government policymakers.

In the bid of the economies in transition to achieve the welfare status of many of the developed western countries, it was naturally disappointing to have rather been subjected to a so-called transitional recession, which, although expected, was rather deep, long, and persistent[2], making the term *transitional* perhaps unfitting. Real output after the initial years of reform went down so much in many countries that one might be able to conclude that the macroeconomic stabilization policies that aim for growth and long-term development, as well as the efforts at increasing the efficiency of enterprises via the removal of the centralized planning system, were largely misguided.

1.1.2 Employment and other social aspects

The shift from central planning to a market-oriented system has put a pressure on the employment sector. This is attributable to the fact that in the old system, there is practically no unemployment; everybody had a job to do. There was no correspondence between the employment contracts and the actual performance of the firms. This is a fundamental structure that is naturally expected to be hit hard by a change to a competitive system, where individual efforts matter in the overall performance of the firms, which in turn determines the formation of employment contracts. Massive layoffs during the transition process should therefore not come as a surprise. However, because of the failure to correctly predict the effects of the macroeconomic policies, as well as the failure to appropriately set up the supporting programs like institution building that is supposed to facilitate the change towards market orientation, the unemployment level was disappointingly worse than expected. This is partly due to the fact that real output has been too low, even lower than the pre-

[2] Economic Commission for Europe (1995) p. 10.

reform periods. Even with the increased private sector activity, this has not been enough to absorb the excess labor under the new system. [3]

The consequence of increased unemployment is increased social unrest, and a consequent disbelief in the market-oriented system, as is now seen in some of the transition economies. This, however, further aggravates the market risk, which in many ways also drives the needed investments away from the country. The other aspect of the low employment level is its effect on the financial status of the government; too low tax revenues and too high expenditures required to support the transition process, which then pulls the economy even further down. With a government that is financially burdened, the social sector is among the first to be affected. Social programs lose priority over other programs. This is to be observed in Russia, where citizens on the social net experience a worsening of their economic condition to a level that might already be classified as being on the brink of starvation.

1.1.3 Investments

The old regime was characterized by an economic system with assets that need a full restructuring to fit into the new market system. Investments from both the government and the private sectors were and still are needed for this restructuring to support the growth objectives. However, with a poorly performing domestic economy, there are very few opportunities for raising the needed investment for the appropriate projects if one limits the options only within the local economy. In addition, there is no functioning domestic capital market that could satisfy the investment demand. Banks are overburdened with bad debts, that additional credit may be too costly or even impossible to obtain. Banks are in any case also in need of reform, and in general could not be a reliable partner for the private investors if the reform has not been undertaken in the banking system. [4]

In this case, foreign investments are considered as one of the fundamental needs of the economies in transition. In the beginning, there was optimism from the point of view of the western companies as to the potentials of the eastern European countries as a market with an abundance of very cheap and skilled labor. This was seen as an

---

[3] Or perhaps one should say that it is rather *because* of the increased private sector activity (which required a correspondence of the employees' productivity to wage and/or employment contract) that unproductive labor were quickly laid off, leading to a rise in unemployment.

[4] see the OECD (1993) report on the reform of the banking system for a more detailed discussion.

4

advantage that could make the western European products competitive in the world market. However, for some reasons, the investments into these countries did not flow as was initially expected. In particular, investments in small scale business were harder to come by.[5] This again was one factor for the negative growth of the economy.

1.1.4 The role of government

In most established market economies, one of the fundamental roles of the government is to safeguard the rights of the individual via the enforcement of established rules and regulations that foster the continued functioning of the market. Such a framework promotes an environment that is conducive to development and growth. Governments who follow this basic tenet must ensure that there is an established effective legal system where property rights are unambiguous, secure, and freely alienable.[6] However, the property rights system that is seen in these established economies are not "put up" by the governments, but rather has evolved in time. If the existing property rights system is a product of market evolution and not of a conscious effort to set it up, there is a need to identify what property rights mean, to be able to define the system that supports it. Under this framework, the notion of property rights can be much too complex for definition.[7]

The situation is different in the transforming economies. The reform process cannot follow the evolutionary path that the established market economies underwent, simply because it takes too much time for the institutions of the legal system to be established in this way to fit into the ideal management of the existing stock of capital and other resources which have been accumulated during the socialist period. The government must thus take an active role in designing an "optimal" institutional framework that will somehow make use of the current resources to support growth within the economy, and at the shortest possible span of time. However, this is not an easy task, and the role of the government is really fuzzy in this area. On the one hand, it is agreed upon by many that an established legal system is necessary to develop and support a well-defined system of property rights. If this is the requirement, then there is an

---

[5] this aspect is very much related to microeconomic problems in privatization and enterprise reform. Among other problems, private companies became reluctant to simply take over the small debt-ridden and unprofitable companies.

[6] Rapaczynski (1996) p. 87.

[7] the next section elaborates on this.

urgent and foremost need to reform the government which will in turn make sure that the correct institutions, as well as its rules and regulations, are set up to be able to enforce the rights of the individual towards the use of their property.[8] On the other hand, it might be the case that the market institutions are really the determinants of the system of property rights, and the legal system's role is simply to put flesh (and stamp) into the market transactions and consequently need only to react to some adjustments in the market. In the latter case, the creation of the government machinery is not too critical, as the market will come up with the appropriate allocation of resources. It follows the sort of evolutionary process that most existing markets

have experienced.[9] The truth might lie somewhere in between, or perhaps having a mixture of both, and it is still necessary to define how the supporting role of the government could be designed to achieve the goals of development. In any case, one can summarize the major argument surrounding the process of transformation to be the divestiture of the state from most economic activities and a move towards a supporting role that promotes the market activities of the private sector.[10]

1.2 Microeconomic issues

The microeconomic issues surrounding the problem of transformation rest on the establishment of functioning and efficient firms that would provide the goods and services needed by the economy. The transformation involves a reallocation of resources in a way that promotes general economic efficiency. But such is best achieved when the individual consumption as well as production activities of the firms are efficient. That the socialists' main distinguishing feature is the dominance of the state sector, the discussion on the microeconomic aspects inevitably requires a comparison of the performance of the state-owned enterprises against the private enterprises. It then becomes necessary to discuss the reasons for the failures of the state-owned enterprises to perform. The issue is, however, anchored on aspects related to efficiency in the use of resources, and is inseparable from the aspects of incentive-

---

[8] but in this case, any form of initial allocation of the resources will be acceptable, and the legal system will just continue to ensure that the ownership structure is respected and the exchange rules enforced.

[9] which means that the market has a "demand" for the services of the government, unlike in the first where the government must firstly supply the framework where the market will conduct its activities.

[10] In chapter 2, a discussion on the existing debate on the role of the government is also presented in the light of the issue of privatization. The discussion includes a review of the arguments based on concepts of nationalization and denationalization schemes.

compatibility in contract formation. In other words, in order to understand the reasons for any divergence between the efficiency levels of the state and the private firms, there is a need to see the incentive structure surrounding the internal organization of the institution that lead the firms and individuals to perform economic activities in a specific manner. In a world of incomplete information, recognizing the requirement to promote an environment that is incentive-compatible to the efficient allocation of resources is the key to the solution of the (in)efficiency problem faced by the policymakers in the transforming economies.

1.2.1 Efficiency of state-owned vs. private enterprises

There are many empirical studies undertaken comparing the efficiency of the state against the private firms in providing goods and services. In most cases, these studies compare the costs of production of the same good between the government and the private firm. The evidence provided is used as a basis for making strong conclusions that the private sector is more efficient than the public sector. Later studies have qualified this statement to also consider the general competitive environment surrounding the firm. As Borcheling, Pommerenhe and Schneider (1982) wrote,[11]

> *The literature seems to indicate that a) private production is cheaper than production in publicly owned and managed firms, and b) given sufficient competition between public and private producers (and no discriminative regulations and subsidies), the differences in unit cost turn out to be insignificant. From this we may conclude that it is not so much the differences in the transferability of ownership but the lack of competition which leads to the often observed less efficient production in public firms.*

Thus private firms can be as (in)efficient as the state enterprises, if the economic environment is such that the choice of the optimal levels of resources (be it labor and other resources) that satisfy their self serving interest lead to sub-optimal levels of resource allocation from the point of view of the society.[12] Competition is the key to efficiency.

Boardman and Vining (1989) on the other hand, claim that in general, state enterprises and mixed enterprises are less profitable and less efficient than private corporations.[13]

---

[11] cited in Bös (1991) p. 51.

[12] one can also refer to this as a case of an imposition of negative externalities to the other agents of the economy, which leads to inefficiency from the point of view of the society.

[13] This was made on the basis of a survey on more than 400 private companies, 57 public enterprises and 23 mixed public-private enterprises.

7

Why this is so has not been elaborated clearly. The study rather focused on the empirical evidence to support the notion that the state is less efficient than the private sector. However, there are other studies that discuss the absence of conclusive, systematic evidence on the relative inefficiency of the public sector.[14] In general, definitive statements based on empirical data cannot be made.

What seems to be rather more interesting is the current empirical evidence on the increased government debt resulting from the financing of the state-owned enterprises (SOEs). There is increasing evidence that the state-owned enterprises almost always operate at a loss. The empirical evidence suggests that the SOEs contribute less to the countries' growth compared to the private sector activities. Countries which have a large proportion of enterprises owned by the state tend to squeeze the private investors out of the capital market, because the heavy demand of the SOEs for capital makes it difficult for the private investors to compete against the government for funding sources, which then leads to other related problems in squeezing out growth in the economy. Vernon (1988) discusses the following to be the main problems connected with the operations of the SOEs:

a) mismanagement, corruption, patronage, and padded payrolls that raised the costs of providing goods and services;

b) inefficient operations, maintenance and service delivery arising in part from weak competition or from monopoly positions;

c) involvement in highly capital intensive operations or investments with long payback periods;

d) constraints on pricing policies by governments wishing to provide subsidized or cheap services for political reasons, preventing the SOEs from recovering their full operating costs;

e) overly restrictive government controls on the budget and finances of the SOEs;

f) failure of the central governments to provide promised subsidies or deliver budgetary resources in a timely manner; and

---

[14] see for example, Milward and Parker (1983).

g) government requirements that SOEs take over failed privately owned businesses or provide inherently unprofitable goods and services.

If these are true, then the dominance of the public sector in the socialist economies produces a situation of general economic inefficiency which at some point in time leads to a collapse of the system, as is the case seen now.

A brief run through this list of problems would lead one to search for a more fundamental explanation on why such things are observed in reality. The fundamental welfare theorem of Arrow and Debreu provide little insight on how this can be addressed, simply because it ignores the fact that the efficiency levels can only be attained through a decision-making process that considers the *incentives* of the agents within an institution to perform certain tasks. Although the incentive structure determines the production and exchange activities in the market, it is also highly dependent on the initial allocation of resources.[15] Thus, it is more precise to say that the incentive structure, given a particular income distribution, determines the types of transactions and contracts formed. This in the end determines the nature of the outcome of the economic activities.

1.2.2 Property rights and incentives

Among the major issues cited in the identification of the requisites to a successful transformation is the establishment of well-defined property rights. In particular, private property is identified to be incentive-compatible to efficiency and thus also to growth and development. It is therefore in the interest of the society to promote it. If it is to be promoted, there must be a consensus as to the meaning of the term. But Waldron (1988) claims that a proper definition of the term "private property" could be elusive, and thus in addition to the attempt to define it, one must identify the conditions whereby it functions. He proposes that (p. 26):

> *If property is indefinable, it cannot serve as a useful concept in political and economic thought... Instead of talking about property systems, we should focus perhaps on the detailed rights that particular people have to do certain things with certain objects, rights which vary considerably from case to case, from object to object, and from legal system to legal system.*

---

[15] or in the same manner, the income distribution.

9

The idea of property should be treated from the point of view of *the assignment of rights* to the use of the resource, be it to private individuals (private property), to the society as a whole (collective property) or to a group of individuals (common property). In the socialist economies, there was one form of property rights which existed, largely of the type *collective* property, in which the state has the legal rights to the decisions on the use and disposal of the assets. If divestiture is the main task of the government in the transformation process, then one can say that this involves a change in the assignment of the property rights from the collective ownership to private ownership.

Another point of view is provided by Grossman and Hart (1986), who define property rights to be the residual control rights over the assets. This definition, however, does not make a distinction between physical rights and legal rights, since it rather focuses on the economic aspects of the property transfer. Schleifer (1994) finds this distinction to be an important consideration in economies in transition. [16] Although the assignment of the residual rights over assets to private individuals improves the incentives in various economic activities involving the use of the asset, the establishment of private property is *necessary* but *not sufficient* to ensure a high level of efficiency in the production process. The government must, in addition, develop a *legal system* which enforces contracts fairly, effectively, and quickly. This appears to be similar to the arguments of Waldron. The actual transfer of the "right" to the private individual is only a first step in the move towards a market-oriented system. If the private individuals are aware of the legal framework under which they could make their decisions on the use of the property, then they can adopt long-term plans that serve their own interests within this given framework. Contracts can be written between the individuals that allow them to undertake activities that are welfare-improving. The assignment of the residual control rights to private individuals, with this legal background, is the key to the achievement of efficiency in the imperfect markets of the transforming economies.

---

[16] He cites as an example a top executive of a corporation who has the physical right to allocate the resources of the firm to their personal advantage although he has no legal right to do so. In transforming economies, the aim should be to make physical rights legal and legal rights physical. Assigning physical and legal rights to property gives an incentive to the executive to use the resources in the interest of the company, which in the end is the same as his interest. Rent-seeking activities are minimized.

1.3 The role of privatization in transforming economies[17]

To put flesh into the idea of property rights transfer, many governments have adopted the implementation of a privatization program as one of its priorities. Divestiture is considered as a necessary activity that the government should undertake in aiming for sustainable growth objectives (Schleifer and Vishny, 1994).

Privatization under the general framework of transforming economies is defined by Inotai (1992) and Hax (1991) as a process of transferring public resources to private owners, with a view of bringing in a change in the structure of ownership necessary to create *firms* which can stand on their own in a market environment, to stimulate investment, and create entrepreneurial incentives. It is by now generally accepted to be a key element in the process of transformation that aims to achieve some specified goals, which among others include efficiency, revenue generation, employment stabilization, equity, and political stability.

1.3.1 The task involved.

Although privatization has been identified to be necessary from the very beginning of the transition process, this is still an activity that keeps most of the governments busy. The task is difficult and sometimes complicated, as the privatization program is not limited to a simple transfer of resources from public to private hands, as was previously discussed. The fact that the privatization process is to be undertaken in the light of long-term development objectives of the economies in transition requires a careful thought on the appropriate design that is fitting for these economies. In principle, it should be different from the privatization activities so far undertaken in the established western markets.

The size and extent of the accumulated resources that is included in the privatization program makes the whole activity one of great political interest, not only for the policy makers, but for various interest groups that undertake rent-seeking activities. Note that the majority, if not all of the resources were either controlled or outright confiscated by the state, leaving the state the single most powerful unit that determines the use and disposal of the resources during the socialist era. In the privatization process, however,

---

[17] This section provides only an overview of the problem in relation to transformation. An extensive discussion on privatization is presented in the following chapter.

11

such a monopoly position for a state consisting of many individuals of varying levels of interest proves to be a factor that contributes to the complexity of the design process. In the decision to undertake privatization, the state has to suddenly consider the general public in its planning activity, and this in itself is a new phenomenon that they have to firstly get used to. In the process of learning, there is a danger of being pulled into activities in various different directions that may or may not be misguided even with the best of intentions. On the other hand, they may also take the freedom to undertake rent-seeking activities as long as the environment is fuzzy enough to allow them to do this discreetly.

In established markets, there is a long list of reference to rent-seeking activities conducted by the politicians in undertaking activities that involve the design of institutions that give themselves extensive political control. In some cases, although it may appear that they have relegated the physical property rights to private individuals, they exercise continued control of the resources through the establishment of various institutional schemes. This seems to be a point of similarity between the two markets. In implementing the privatization programs, the governments have to go through a rough sailing to overcome problems of corruption, misrepresentation of information and other related matters that lead to both design problems, implementation and enforcement of the rules and regulations in the privatization program.

1.3.2 Policies and goals.

All privatization activities have been shown to be undertaken *without* a single sustained rationale. Bishop and Kay (1992) claims that governments set multiple objectives[18] in the conduct of privatization. By the nature of how such objectives are set, these cannot be achieved consistently as originally aimed at. Trade-offs are predominantly observed, and political aims often come in the forefront before any economic needs. Gray (1996) has identified the following as the three main goals of privatization programs in the transforming economies:

---

[18] Inotai (1992) enumerates some of the most important goals targeted in privatization programs: efficiency, revenue generation, employment stabilization, equity, political stability. For the particular problem of privatization in transforming economies, it is not only the much-emphasized efficiency that is an important objective to achieve. *Equity* is as important, if not more important a consideration in the conduct of the privatization process. However, although efficiency could be neatly defined in standard microeconomic analysis, no standard objective definition could be provided for equity. (see Savoie, Donald and Irving Brecher , 1992) This becomes even more difficult, as explicit objectives of the government in the transition process relate to equity aspects, among others, in the design of institutional change.

a) Creating "real" owners.

Gray refers to this as the process of creation of the true representatives of capital who reap the benefits from any improvement in the economic efficiency.[19] In essence, she zeros in on the creation of the incentive structures that stimulate the infusion of capital, technology, ideas, and skills that complement the changes in the economic and institutional structure of the transforming economies. Thus, evaluating the behavior of the participants in the new economic environment is a key factor that must be considered in the design of the program.

b) Developing supporting institutions

As was previously discussed, the transforming economies need institutions of private market economy. Even in some countries where some private institutions have been established (as in Poland), there is a need to re-orient their activities to face the challenges of competition in an open economy. These institutions also include the legal framework defining property rights, private contract regimes, fiduciary activity, dispute resolution mechanisms, and rules of entry and exit for private firms. However, this also includes the establishment of the basic market ethics that is heavily relied upon by market participants in the Western world.

c) Creating a sustainable reform process

Identifying the single formula for a sustainable reform process is still a difficult task to do. Each of the country has followed more or less a unique concoction of macro and microeconomic policies that aim at a long-term process of steady development. Some key indices that could be referred to in the design of the reform process, however, exist. One of the key points is related again to the incentive structure built upon the institutions that support the broad-based market development. In general, there should be a strong, implementable policy for effective corporate governance that prevents the concentration of economic and political power that is very similar to the old socialist structure being demolished. An example of a failure in this aspect is Russia, where the efforts at reform has created a general feeling of distrust and resentment on the part of the citizenry towards any further reform, simply because there are only a very small, selected number of insiders who became very rich in the process of reform. If this is seen to be widespread, then the ethical standards of the reform take a shape that might

---

[19] But also should bear the burden in taking risks if the activity fails.

not have been intended to be created, as is now seen in Russia. The point is, there must be some commitment from the side of the government to implement true reforms by severing the old links between the firms and ministries, say , in the form of pervasive subsidies that coddle the firms and prevent general restructuring. Confidence in the market and the reform process lead to a steady, even if slow, growth of investment and capital available. The speed of implementation is, however, not necessarily the requirement to achieve such.

To summarize, the whole issue of transformation is not an easy task for the governments of the ex-socialist countries to undertake. Nobody can really claim to have the necessary knowledge to push for a reform process that promotes a steady increase in the welfare of the people in these economies. However, there are fundamental aspects that many agree to be important in pushing for a reform process, whether the reform is a big bang or gradual reform. The most important of these is the creation of an incentive structure that promotes efficient economic activities to be undertaken by the private sector in the market. Although privatizing the state-owned assets is the core task in this respect, the institutional framework that supports this private sector-led economy must also be put in place in order to guarantee a stable reform to a market economy.

2. Privatization: Concept, theory, issues and experiences

Privatization was earlier in this paper defined[20] as the transfer of property rights from the collective to private individuals. Thus the form of property ownership is transformed from being *public* to being *private*. Many countries have embarked on privatization programs for reasons that vary along with the differences in the structure of the implementing countries and economies. The most active pioneers are France and Britain. Interesting theoretical and empirical researches have already been conducted on the two countries' experiences in this direction, and since many of these studies provide positive feedback on the idea of privatization, other Western as well as Asian countries are following suit. West Germany, Austria, Belgium and other European countries which have large nationalized enterprises have also already embarked on such a program.

In the years before the breakdown of the socialist economies, researches on the theory and practice of privatization have centered mainly on the activities in market economies. The analyses reflected the outstanding issues and problems in established economies, as well as the positive effects of privatizing in terms of increasing the welfare of the society. In general, these privatization activities were based on sound theoretical justification. In the transforming economies, the issue of privatization has taken a major role in the efforts to become a full-fledged market economy. The theoretical arguments for privatization used are much the same as before, although with some qualifications in the economic environment within the transforming economies. In general, it has been established that privatization in transforming economies, much the same as in established market economies, is a beneficial activity. It provides a positive contribution to the economies in the form of, among others, increased welfare to the society.[21]

Privatization could be done partially or wholly. In the former, the government maintains a certain percentage share in the ownership of the resource or an enterprise,

---

[20] There are many ways by which the concept of privatization is defined. See Thiemeyer (1986) for a discussion on several concepts of privatization. Cited in Bös (1991)

[21] But it remains to be noted that although it is necessary, it is not sufficient for a successful transformation.

while in the latter, complete ownership is given to private individuals. Such a transfer of ownership is justified on the basis of its economic as well as political desirability. It is economically desirable because, as was earlier claimed, it promotes an increase in the welfare of the individuals in the society. On the other hand, it is politically desirable because it promotes democratization.

With the change in the ownership of the resources, adjustments are brought upon not only in economic but also in political as well as social, institutional and legal aspects. Thus, a discussion on privatization will be incomplete without these other aspects. This chapter surveys the justification cited for privatization in general, how it is implemented so far in transforming economies, and the preliminary results following the initial efforts. Finally, the issues surrounding the land privatization program are discussed to put the research in perspective, and as an introduction to the following chapter on the objectives and scope of the study.

2.1 Reasons for Privatization

We describe hereunder some apparent reasons used as basis for privatization. The classification of these arguments is similar to that discussed in Bös (1991), i.e., political and economic reasons. The former is expanded to include social reasons.

2.1.1 Political and social reasons.

The transfer of resources from the government[22] to private hands involves not only a redistribution of wealth and income, but also of the opportunities and power attached to the possession of these resources. In economy-wide privatization involving the transfer of the property rights of a number of companies, big and small, many of these economies' citizens are affected by the outcome of the process. Politicians, bureaucrats, managers, employees, consumers, traders, etc., whether or not they participate directly in the process, either influence it or get affected by it. Large-scale privatizations not only have microeconomic effects within the privatized firms, but also macroeconomic effects.

---

[22] Some authors are reluctant to say "public" instead of government, as this word is also sometimes a source of confusion. After all, the "public" is a collection of individuals in the society.

Economic power, sometimes referred to as capitalistic power, steers political power, at least in many established market economies.[23] The transfer of large amounts of resources/assets via privatization affects the distribution of power via the transfer of political control, or call it *clout*, from the bureaucrats to the private owners, shareholders, or managers. This is then to say that whosoever has the *de facto* rights to control a considerable stock of resources has in his hands the corresponding political power. This is perhaps the reason why a number of large enterprises in established markets are reluctant to privatize. Instead of privatization, the managers and employees support reorganization schemes which would still maintain the power structure and control by the key people involved in the decision making process.

In the ex-socialist countries, privatization is seen to involve a devolution of decision-making from the central government. There is a complete overhaul in the economic and political system which results in a restructured power base. This goes as well with the bureaucratic machinery that drives this system. The political essence of privatization in both economies is thus quite similar: a decentralized power structure. The transfer of the power to control the use and disposal of resources leads to the transfer of political power to the common man. Since the common man, who compose the majority, gets the right to the ownership of the resources, the so-called *people's capitalism* is promoted, instead of capitalism by a few. Such is a politically palatable argument that is not difficult to sell to the majority of the people, and is as a consequence, one of the most frequently cited reasons for privatization.

Following this argument, in both western and the ex-socialist countries, privatization is in most cases undertaken with the idea to disperse the ownership as wide as possible. One very appealing concept adopted is that those who have a modest income should also be able to participate even in a modest amount. As in a democratic society, no single individual could control the economy via the control of his own share of the resources. However, the collective would, and this collective power could be strengthened in the privatization process if the resources are dispersed wide enough.[24]

It is admittedly sometimes difficult to draw a clear line between economic, political and social power. Indeed, these are very much intertwined in a capitalistic world. As

---

[23] those who have the means could, say, possibly buy themselves into power.

[24] This is sometimes an argument for mass privatization whereby the assets are distributed to the general public via certificates of ownership of shares of large units of assets, but without payment to the government.

previously argued, political power has a sound foundation on economic power in a capitalistic economy. The German trade union has a considerable influence in the policies that determine the fate of the country's economy. This clout rests on their success in securing continued gains for and on behalf of the employees they represent. Bös (1991) cites that they oppose any privatization because of the fear that the employees will lose their privileges, in which case they lose the confidence of the individuals they represent. In addition, the union's political power rests on, among others, the collective character of the employees whose objectives are to maximize their income and social status. The *Deutsche Bahn* and the *Bundespost* employees enjoyed a civil servant status; the job of a civil servant is coveted and aspired for by many in the country. A civil servant status gives the employees more economic power (because it is paid well), and raise their social as well as political status. Privatization takes this privilege away from them, and is thus expectedly opposed. This despite the fact that the rest of the society expects to gain from the program.

The government's role in a democratic society is mainly centered on ensuring that the society achieves its goals, which in a broad sense could be defined as the improvement of the social welfare of the people. However, how such is implemented and how the activities are prioritized depend very much on who the leaders are and what type of government in power is. In most cases, the goals that the government pursues are constantly changing and highly subject to political and social pressures of the most influential voting block. The extent to which actual decisions on the use and disposal of resources are made need not be in agreement with the pronounced goal of maximizing the welfare of the general public. The interest of the most influential political and/or social group is in general taken into consideration. This is why it is argued that it is very dangerous to leave the management of enterprises in the hands of the government, who has no stable objective to base its activities on. Private enterprises are less subject to the vagaries of political and social pressures.[25] People accept that the latter have to work under the principle of profit maximization, but the former must always serve the interest of the people. But the interest of the society is rather variable across different groups. The society is composed of several different groups with differing opinions and goals to pursue. More often than not, whosoever is loudest in conveying these interests to the government is the one heard and represented. The government's tendency is to work more on problem areas which i

---

[25] Notable exceptions such as multinational corporations, however, exist.

quickly identifies via these political or pressure groups. The privatization activities are not exempt from it.

2.1.2 Economic Reasons

A very popular economic justification for privatization is the *efficiency* of the private sector in the management of assets/resources. In the case of production, Higgins (1992) defines industry or firm efficiency as that involving the maximization of the unit's contribution to development, or in increase in welfare, which are equivalent. In neoclassical economics, economic efficiency refers to a condition of Pareto optimality, which has the characteristic of both productive and allocative efficiency. Productive efficiency (or sometimes called technological efficiency) in the neoclassical sense involves the maximization of the output produced from the inputs using the available technology. Thus Higgins's definition is based on the productive efficiency of a firm. Allocative efficiency, on the other hand, refers to a situation whereby the supply of resources within the economy, both for production and consumption purposes, is allocated across industries and activities such that these contribute to the maximization of the society's welfare. It is achieved when the prices in the market are set "correctly" such that the market activities lead to the so-called general equilibrium. In short, for allocative efficiency to be achieved, the prices of the resources should reflect the correct rates of returns, thus leading to an efficient allocation within the economy.

Bös (1991) supports the earlier claim (chapter 1) of this paper that there are a host of empirical studies showing that privately run enterprises are more technologically efficient than their state-run counterparts.[26]

But as was earlier indicated, discussions on the concepts relating to efficiency, both productive as well as allocative, will be insufficient without the discussion on incentives. After all, the driving force that makes private firms more efficient compared to their state-run counterparts in a market economy is mainly anchored on the incentives that the agents within the institutions have. Any program of privatization should always look at the incentive structure before and after the process, if efficiency is a key objective to be achieved. Since incentives in the micro level translates to

---

[26] In as far as the contribution of inputs to the production process is concerned, Murrell (1992) shows that there is very little difference between the efficiency of the state enterprises in socialist countries as against private enterprises in Western countries.

macro level effects[27] more especially so in a large scale privatization, the structure of incentives in the micro level must be consistent with macro level objectives targeted.

The traditional macro principles emphasize the importance of the role of the state in stabilizing the economy, especially in periods of temporary recessions. In the extreme case, Keynesian economics argue for increased intervention of the government in terms of increased public expenditures to get the economy out of the "liquidity trap" and lead the economy back to the normal levels of economic activity. If this is so, then nationalization instead of privatization would be a good program to support, as it provides enough room for the government to conduct expansionary activities that would pump prime the economy. In reality, however, the government is not always prudent enough and is also liable to commit errors, both on the prediction and the assessment of which conditions require heavy interventions. The fact that the government can never possess good enough quality and quantity of information could lead to intervention errors that may be more destructive rather than constructive to the ailing economy that it aims to help. The Chicago Rational Expectations economists have tried to provide theoretical foundations to this. They have claimed that in the long run, these interventions are not at all curative of the economies' ailing; these are rather more distortionary than stabilizing. Based on this argument, the government should keep its hands off the market which anyway will take care of itself. It should not venture into activities in which private initiatives are also possible and observable. Privatization of enterprises instead of nationalization should be encouraged.

The literature on public economics also argues for similar ideas. Government intervention in the form of the provision of public goods or publicly provided private goods should only be undertaken in cases where there is a market breakdown. If there is indeed a market breakdown, direct provision by the government is not always the optimal response to the situation. Regulatory mechanisms could also be undertaken, allowing the private sector to own the enterprises or own the assets/ resources, with government regulatory support. This is normally an argument for firms which are natural monopolies.[28]

---

[27] and vice-versa.

[28] see Laffont and Tirole (1994) for interesting discussions on the theory of regulations.

In several papers[29], the problem of transformation of the financial sector is shown to be very much intertwined with the problem of the privatization of the state enterprises. The financial sector is a strong link that binds the microeconomic and the macroeconomic conditions. In this case, the state of the financial market has an important role in the whole economic system and the success potentials in the transforming economies. However, the financial sector is also burdened with transformation problems of its own. One major problem in this sector, particularly in the banking sector, is related to the existence of bad debts which have been carried over by the state enterprises from the past regime. These state enterprises have pre-reform debts which it could not pay anymore, given the new conditions it faces in the market economy. The lender, the state commercial banks, hold a significant part of its portfolio in the form of these bad debts. Despite the continuous unprofitable operations of the state enterprises, these state banks continue to lend to them, and the result is an uncontrolled increase in the amount of defaults, a lock-in situation which could perpetuate without a sweeping reform. The problem also becomes a chicken-and-egg question. The state enterprises continue to be coddled and become more inefficient, which makes it extremely difficult to privatize. The banks are no different than their clients, and a privatization becomes difficult if the bad debts are not properly addressed. The magnitude of the debt drags the economy down, and the rest of the enterprises face difficulties to find private investors.

Many of the existing large enterprises in transforming economies are still managed by the state. They operate with huge losses that continue to be financed by the government with the luxury of a secure source of budget for its activities, largely coming from general fund taxation. A similar private firm facing heavy losses would immediately face the threat of foreclosure. Hard budget constraints in the case of the state owned-enterprises are rarely, if at all, implemented. In addition, the commercial banks continue to be burdened with increasing debts which have no hope of repayment. If privatization becomes possible, say via a sale coupled with some radical reforms, this could lead to a larger available budget pie by eliminating the deficit financing, by contributing directly to the revenues collected by the government and by enlarging the tax base created by the effects of freeing some financial assets for other

---

[29] see OECD (1993) for more on financial sector reforms.

more profitable enterprises.[30] However, it could not be done without dealing with the existing debt problems.

The human resources component is another aspect that should also not be put aside, as the ultimate productivity of the enterprises is determined by the productivity of the workers. The human resources need to undergo a transformation of its own kind to respond properly to the demands of a functioning market institution. Here, the incentive problems resurface once again, in the form of investments in human resource development that is more responsive to the market-oriented structure evolving out of the transformation process.

The problem in transforming economies is much more complex and serious than could be imagined. In the limited area of the problem of privatization, the continued possession of the enterprises by the state means that continued financing has to be provided from the general fund taxation. The longer the ex-socialist governments hold on to the state resources, the longer they hold on to the burden of financial responsibility, and the greater is the burden transferred indirectly to the people since other services that should be provided by the government become scarce.

In traditional microeconomic analysis, efficiency is achieved when the market is allowed to operate freely in the sense of Adam Smith's invisible hand. Markets are, however, rarely (or not at all) perfectly competitive, such that the efficiency condition in the neo-classical sense will hardly be observed. The market, when allowed to work freely, can have prices which fail to reflect the equality between value in use and value in exchange. Thus, one reason cited for government intervention is in the case of a market breakdown, where the market fails to operate because of the inability of the prices to reflect the true opportunity cost of using the resources in the production of the goods traded, as in a situation with externalities in production and/or consumption.

Public goods, which are characterized by externalities in the form of jointness in consumption, nonrivalry and non-excludability, will not be provided by any profit-oriented private firm. Although there is a positive benefit to the society in providing the good, the free-riding problem takes away the incentive to produce it. In general, the solution offered is for the government to provide such goods. The government, however, has to figure out the right price to charge each of the consumers, to ensure

---

[30] To a certain extent, leasing also achieves the same by allowing the private individuals to shoulder the financial as well as managerial responsibilities of running the enterprises.

that the public good is efficiently provided, in the sense that the cost of the good is equal to the sum of the marginal rates of substitutions of the consumers.[31] The existence of this type of externality makes it difficult for any private firm to be encouraged towards its production, unless under some special regulatory environments or special programs to allow the firm to recover its cost and end up with some rent.[32] For these goods, there is thus an economic argument for the government to continue to provide such goods, or to continue ownership of goods with external economies.[33]

2.1.3 Normative economic arguments.

The above discussions have centered mainly on positive economic arguments. The other aspect has reference to arguments based on normative economic criteria. Here lies some definitional difficulties on the reasons for undertaking privatization. Some normative goals may include fairness, justice, and equity. The problem is, no satisfactory theory can provide a standard definition of these normative goals. It is even more problematic in the light of transforming economies[34].

Justice. It is argued that privatization in transforming economies needs to be undertaken because it promotes justice. Many of the state enterprises/ resources actually came originally from private hands. These were acquired by the government mostly via the confiscation of the assets during the socialist regimes and the transfer is done by force,[35] against the will of the former owners. A return of these assets to their rightful owners is considered just. A question arises as to whether the government currently in charge is able to design a fair and equitable process by which to return these assets. Indeed, for many transforming economies, restitution has been adopted as one of the priority mechanisms for privatization. This is however, possible only when no legal and/or physical problems exist in establishing the ownership of the assets. In many cases, restitution is not possible, and so some other mechanism of privatization must also be considered.

---

[31] or equivalently, to their willingness to pay.

[32] As in build-operate-transfer (BOT) programs.

[33] As in the ownership of public roads and bridges.

[34] a discussion on the theoretical definitions appears in the next section.

[35] Of course within the framework of the communist law, so at the time of the confiscation, this act was considered to be legal.

Equity. Higgins (1992) argues that the closest definition to equity is *equality*:

> *" equity means not permitting greater inequalities of income, wealth, power, privilege, and social status than a society should".*

It is clear from this statement that in order to properly define equity, there is a need to understand equality, or perhaps more precisely, inequality. Equality may be defined in various ways. It can refer to absolute equality in the sense of having absolutely no difference in wealth, status, power, and privilege. But this state of the world obviously does not exist, and the argument can be considered as invalid; equity is pure tautology in this case. On the basis of Higgin's definition, the status quo seems to be very important. If one has absolute equality, then equity means that any change that takes place in the economy, whether it is an increase or a decrease (in wealth, income) should be equally divided such that the status quo remains undisturbed. If there is no absolute equality, then some *inequalities* exist, but the status quo need not be maintained, because the change that the society allows will depend on how much inequality can be tolerated, as can be verified by the last word *should* in Higgin's statement. In other words, a change that is *intolerable* to the society in terms of the distribution of increments in income, wealth, power, etc., *should not* be undertaken. But what is intolerable requires an assessment of intensities of preferences of the individuals in the society, which, as has been established in social choice theory, is difficult to undertake.[36]

Fairness. The concept can be linked with the general acceptance of rules governing the distributional increases or decreases in wealth, income, power, etc. Thus, it is related to equity, but is more fundamentally based on the *process* of distribution vis-à-vis the norms accepted. Like equity, it suffers from problems in standardized definitional form. A fair allocation respects the status quo distribution, but requires rather an *individual* assessment of the process, that is, whether it is acceptable or not to the individual on the basis of established norms, and preferences, but again, requiring somehow some comparison of intensities of these preferences.

This as a background, the research simplifies the normative aspect of equity by focusing on the aspects of *equality* in the opportunities provided by a privatization process. Fairness comes in the ability of the program to design rules that allow the

---

[36] Arrow's (1953) essay on the impossibility theorem provides the basic framework of the problem of social choice.

participants to exercise their freedom of choice, respecting their own private decisions, but at the same time allowing the market to find its own path of development with less distortionary interventions from the state. This does not mean that the government should totally refrain from regulatory policies especially if these are highly desirable in terms of guaranteeing a long-term increase in the welfare of the people. The argument, rather, is to promote a program that transfers the property rights in a way that guarantees the eventual owners of the asset their normal, regular democratic rights, just like any other citizen; to exercise this in their economic decision-making using their resources, within the general framework of law existing for a democratic and capitalistic society. For a privatization program to be equitable, it should provide equal opportunities to all, regardless of their status, in terms of realizing some economic gains from the resource transfer. Thus, this basic idea rather refers to the ex ante conditions set by the government in the conduct of the privatization process. A fair privatization process does not discriminate unduly any individual or groups of individual in any of the aspects constituting the rules and regulations of the privatization.[37]

2.2 Other theories of privatization

2.2.1 Economic

The theory of agency. Although many aspects of the real-world privatization process could be very difficult to model formally, the agency theory provides a rich source of ideas that could promote the understanding of the properties of a privatization process. In general, privatization can be seen as a bargaining situation between two agents who possess varying degrees of available information that is also private. The theory looks closely at the economic incentives that drive these agents to do what they do in an environment of incomplete and asymmetric information[38].

Privatization is a case of a principal-agent problem. In the extreme example of the sale of state properties, the asymmetric nature of the information makes it difficult for the state to ensure that each sale conducted will lead to a net increase in social welfare, or

---

[37] For instance, the land privatization program in Germany could be seen to be unfair because it offers the land to a certain group of individuals at a discounted rate.

[38] More on the types of information in chapter 4.

whether it will give the government the highest revenue, if that is the objective. Neither is there any assurance that the awardee will be the most efficient agent in using the state resources bought. If the objective is to maximize society's economic welfare in the privatization process, it is in the interest of the state to make sure that all publicly owned resources be used more effectively and efficiently by the new owners, compared to the state. On top, it must be that the new owner can offer the best technology to promote efficiency in the use of resources, compared to all other interested/prospective bidders.

In order to do this, the state needs information about the type of the interested buyers. That is, he needs to establish who is the most efficient of all possible applicants. To do this requires information on, among others, technological aspects in the use of the resource, conditions in the input as well as in the output markets, and their future developments. Each bidder will have some unique prognosis of the present as well as the future conditions in the market, as well as the best technology available for their foreseen farm business, even if this information is imperfect. But since this is private information to the bidders, it will entail enormous costs to collect this information, if it is possible to collect at all. However, no bidder would want to reveal any information to the seller if he knows it will be used against him, or if he does not gain anything from it. Alternatively, the state could design a privatization mechanism that is incentive-compatible to the buyers telling the truth about the information of interest to the state.[39]

Although the design of the mechanism of privatization is in itself a principal-agent problem, it is also a solution to a particular principal agent problem. The key issue centers on the role of incentive structure in driving the economic activities that are formed within and between contracts. To see this, imagine an extreme case of a three level-contract between the state agricultural enterprise and the directors, and between the directors and the field agricultural workers, who are all employed as civil servants with a fixed salary from the government.

The workers. The workers have the task of performing the field operations needed in the production of the crops and livestock. In this environment, the utility-maximizing agricultural workers will have the tendency to minimize efforts to work (as working is a disutility). Because they have fixed wages, there need not be any correspondence

---

[39] In the literature, this refers to the "type" of the agent. More on this in the theory of mechanism design.

between the efforts they put in to produce output, and the wages that they receive.[40] As long as they have a contract which entitles them to a fixed salary for life, they need not exert too much effort to ensure the highest production they can achieve.[41]

The Directors. The directors have the task of ensuring that the output is at the optimum, and they should undertake monitoring activities to verify the states of nature. They know the technology, and on the basis of this information, they can make inferences on the effort exerted based on the observation of the actual level of the output. However, if they are again on fixed salary for life, there is no incentive to exert a high effort to monitor. If the laborers know this, the situation becomes worse, because then they know that their efforts do not matter to the directors anyway.

The state. The state, in turn, has the job of ensuring that the fields are kept productive, such that the population has enough supply of food. But the state is composed of again, utility-maximizing individuals whose income is independent of the output produced. They would therefore minimize monitoring the activities of the directors, as to do so decreases their utility. Nobody monitors them, except perhaps the general public. But they are not elected, and so there is no need to worry about what the general public says, as the state will remain the state, and the individuals will keep their jobs as civil servants.

The process goes on. In the end, production becomes inefficient, because the effort in each level is not monitored, imperfectly observed, or is simply not observed. The environment is, in general, not incentive compatible for increasing the output. This is the fundamental reason which is believed to be the core problem in ex-socialist economies, which led to the inefficiency and the eventual breakdown of the state enterprises.

In a democratic society, one could imagine that politicians take more responsibility in monitoring (i.e., compared to their socialist counterparts) because their term of office is determined by how well they are able to do their job of ensuring the improved welfare of the citizenry. Since monitoring of political actions could also only be

---

[40] see Shapiro and Stiglitz (1984)

[41] To the extent that there are variables other than efforts and material inputs that affect the level of the output, say, weather, there will be some uncertainty as to the actual contribution of the labor units to the total production. There is a problem of moral hazard with hidden action, wherein the effort cannot be used as a basis of the contract on account of its unobservability. A fixed wage aggravates the problem, because it should in principle be used only when the effort is directly observable. More on moral hazard concepts in chapter 4.

imperfectly enforced, it is possible that politicians put less emphasis on the importance of monitoring the state enterprises. For highly political enterprises[42], there is indeed some pressure for the politicians to be more concerned with the efficiency of the enterprises.

One possible solution to this problem is privatization. If the ownership of land and the agricultural enterprise is transferred to private hands, there is a change in the *residual claimant*. Instead of the state, a private individual will run the agricultural enterprise. Assume that he bought the land. By deciding to buy the land, he conveys that he *expected* to have some positive payoff in farming, the cost of buying the land inclusive. Because the profits of the firm accrue to himself only, it will be in his best interest to undertake activities that will ensure that the profits in the cultivation of the land is maximized.

Note that privatization also creates another P-A problem. In the example, this arises between the new owner and the existing directors. Suppose firstly that the principal keeps the directors in the firm on the same payment scheme as before. The problem of the principal now is to design the conditions under which the directors will have every incentive to do their job to monitor and manage the agricultural workers, such that agricultural activities are undertaken accordingly. The solution is to invest in monitoring, or devise a contract under which the directors also become part of the residual claimants to the firm. Given that the directors have the incentive to do their job, the P-A problem between the directors and the workers remains. But with the increased incentive to monitor, the agricultural workers will be forced to do a better job, or be fired.

In general, the following special features of the P-A relation provide the reasons for the existence of the problem.[43]

a) The asymmetry of precontractual beliefs leads to a problematic situation in determining incentive-compatible contract terms and division of payoffs. This arises from the fact that not all possible contingencies could be fully anticipated in the contract.

---

[42] such as perhaps power, telecoms, and in some cases, steel enterprises.

[43] Sappington (1991) , p.48

b) The level of risk aversion on the part of the agent requires sharing of risk between the principal and the agent to arrive at an optimal contract.

c) The presence of transaction costs[44] affects the behavior of agents to a large extent. Even if a contract is agreed upon, there are possible costs in the enforcement of the terms of the contract. The agent could, at any point in time, renege on the agreement.[45] No single contract can guarantee perfect commitment on the part of both the principal and the agents. This is the classic case of an example of the saying „promises are meant to be broken", and the party which did not renege have to bear the cost.

d) The agent's performance is not subject to perfect observation. If observation could be undertaken at no cost, then there will be no problem in making an inference on the value of the agent's efforts.

As could perhaps be observed in the preceding discussions, much emphasis has been given on the role of information. In fact, this is perhaps the fundamental contribution of the non-neoclassical theory such as the P-A model to the analysis of bargaining and contract formation.

FA Hayek (1945) was one of the earliest critiques of the "standard" economic model. Already then, he stressed the importance of incorporating informational asymmetries as a problem that must be internalized in the decision-making process. In bargaining, any information on the prices would be the single most important information that one could possess. If one knows the price with certainty, then the bargaining process is concluded. The results are already known prior to the transactions, and no strategic actions are allowed in the process. Hayek argued that it is precisely the information asymmetries that are dealt with in the *process* of price formation. In other words, the price that one observes in the market already reflects the outcome of the bargaining process. Assuming that prices are given overly simplifies the friction between the bargaining agents, and thus fails to shed light to the rise of inefficient situations that are driven by strategic actions on account of having private information. Such are also relevant points to make especially in transforming economies where the markets are still being established, and where the standard market information that one is used to in

---

[44] which is considered to be zero in the neo-classical environment

[45] this is also the moral hazard problem, which is discussed in detail in chapter 4.

an established economy is not available or highly unreliable to use in decision-making processes.

To sum, the argument for the use of privatization rests mainly on the P-A problem in a state setting where no one in the system has the incentive to see to it that the efforts are exerted according to what is expected, thereby leading to cases of inefficiency. Privatization changes the residual claimant from the state (or country composed of many disinterested individuals) to a private individual and therefore changes the incentive structure. Although privatization can solve one particular problem of P-A relation, more often, it creates another type of P-A problem between the new principal and the agent. The environment in this new setting is, however, much more incentive-compatible to a formation of an efficient contract between the parties, which promotes general economic welfare, and thus provides a good basis to undertake privatization.

2.2.2 Legal

Andreff (1992) discusses the importance of looking at the legal aspects on the transfer of property rights over the assets. A full privatization, he claims, also involves the transfer of three rights to the owners of the asset: a) right to utilize the assets (*usus*); b) the right to appropriate any returns to the asset (*usus fructus*); and c) the right to transfer the assets and to dispose of property (*abusus*). He claims that if the owners of the assets do not enjoy all these three rights, then privatization has not been fully accomplished. Privatization that only promotes the withdrawal of the state in the activities is not a genuine privatization. He cites leasing as a withdrawal of the state from the activities that involve the use of the assets (*usus*), and the appropriation of the returns to the assets (*usus fructus*), but not the disposition of the assets (*abusus*). A full control of the resource has not been awarded to the private individuals. This applies to denationalization schemes such as self-managed enterprises, which do not constitute privatization in the sense discussed. These of course constitute a load of debates on the issues of property rights. From the economic perspective, it matters which rights are attached to the ownership of the resource. But the rights to the ownership in the real world are defined on the basis of established legal as well as social institutions.[46]

---

[46] As is discussed in chapter 1, section 1.3.2, the development of supporting institutions is one of the key activities in the process of transformation. These institutions include the legal system that protects the property rights.

2.2.3 Regulation

Regulation is justified in most literature when there is an apparent need to reduce and contain the market power of a certain enterprise large enough to effect some changes in the market. There are varying opinions about the role of regulation in ensuring the efficiency of the enterprise being regulated. In transforming economies, some argue that not only should the privatization program per se be regulated to avoid problems of say, corruption, but it is to be used as a tool to direct the activities of the privatized enterprises towards what is seen by the state to be in conjunction with the society's objective function.

Regulatory instruments are used to improve the efficiency of the regulated firm. In the absence of regulation, some privatized firms which remain to be or developed to be a monopoly will perform production activities that extract a high rent which perpetuates the existence of inefficiency. On the other hand, other firms require these regulations to ensure that they keep on existing, because this will be in the interest of the society. There are cases when the product of the firm involves the production of other external products which also benefit consumers other than those directly paying. In the latter, one achieves both productive and allocative efficiency of the potential monopolist, but in the former, it is not sure whether there will be a net positive effect on the society in terms of efficiency, simply because trade-offs might exist in the sense that high prices might have to be traded against productivity increases that could result from full privatization.

On the theoretical level, one can argue that regulatory instruments can be seen to solve some of the problems that are also inherent in P-A relationships, like moral hazard and adverse selection. Regulation is also an agency problem, and thus regulatory instruments may be effective if designed from the point of view of asymmetric information and incentive structures within the regulated firm. However, as is discussed in the legal issues of privatization, there are tendencies to overregulate industries in the sense of too much (or too many) restrictions, which cast doubts on whether full privatization is achieved. Overregulation due to poor information and faulty design of the instruments may dampen the positive effects of the transfer of the property rights to the private individual, which may also result in more inefficiency than in the case of no privatization. In any case, regulatory mechanisms are implemented in conjunction with the law; in transforming economies, privatized assets which are highly political (such as land) are almost always tied with some new regulatory laws limiting the rights to the use and disposal of the asset in question.

2.3 Methods of privatization

There are many ways by which privatization in various different countries has been implemented. Various authors have spent their time and efforts to analyze these methods; how effective these are, and how these relate with the achievement of the espoused objective of the government. But because of the highly politicized nature of this activity, it is not really possible to make a clear-cut statement nor a definitive conclusion as to the effects of one option compared to another. Besides, since there is only a short period of time which has elapsed since the privatization process, it is not possible to evaluate objectively the long-term effects of the privatization programs. At best, these can be judged on the basis of achieving some short-term goals which can have a long-term bearing on the welfare of the society.

Table 2.1 presents a summary of the different methods used so far in transforming economies.

Table 2.1 Methods of privatization

Method of privatization	Procedure	Options	Features	Use in transforming economies
1. Public offering of shares	■ fixed price sale ■ tender ■ stock flotations	■ domestic ■ international ■ restriction on size of individual shareholders or foreigners' part ■ offerings underwritten	■ substantial revenue ■ widespread holding ■ openness and transparency of procedures ■ strong dependence on the primary market (or market substitute) ■ need to restructure loss-making enterprises	Hungary and Poland
2. Private sale of shares	■ bidding, with pre-qualification of bidders ■ direct negotiation	■ domestic ■ international ■ restriction on size of individual shareholders or foreigners' part ■ possible use in conjunction with public offerings	■ discretionary procedure ■ lack of transparency ■ feasible alternative in underdeveloped equity market	Czech Rep. Slovak Rep. Poland Former GDR
- Reorganization into component parts	■ break-up into several legal entities ■ transformation into a holding company sale of productive facilities in single units or groups.	■ sale by parts restructuring: negotiated/sectoral	■ flexibility ■ potential investors more attracted by parts than aggregate ■ allows use of different methods for different components ■ breaking of (potential) monopolies	

33

Method of privatization	Procedure	Options	Features	Use in transforming economies
3. Sale of government or enterprise assets	■ competitive bidding ■ auction ■ direct negotiation	■ sold privately ■ contributed by government to new company with private sector ■ assets sold individually ■ together as a new corporate entity	- assets sold without correspondent liability	Czech Rep. Slovak Rep.
4. New private investment in SOE or debt-equity swaps	■ capital increase (equity ownership open to the private sector	■ public offering of subscription ■ private offer ■ various class of shares ■ new issue and offering of existing government shares	■ funding problems of undercapitalized enterprises ■ generally no sales proceeds for state ■ new funds used for rehabilitation and restoration of working capital ■ extension of SOE capital without state divestment	Hungary
5. Management/employee buy-out	■ creation of a holding company through an equity issue subscribed by management and employees ■ holding company acquires SOE to be privatized		■ main alternative to liquidation ■ need for large (projected) cash flow or other security	■ present in some forms in all countries, esp. in privatization of retail trade ■ Estonia ■ former GDR ■ Poland ■ former Yugoslavia ■ Russia
a) Management buy-out (MBO)	■ acquisition of a		■ rent or leasing of assets	

Method of privatization	Procedure	Options	Features	Use in transforming economies
b) Leveraged management/ employee buy-out (LBO)	controlling shareholding by group of managers ■ acquisition financed by credit		■ buy-out team obtains large share of the equity, providing small portion of funding	■ Czech Rep. ■ Slovak Rep. ■ Romania
c) Employee stock ownership plan (ESOP)	■ employee acquires block of shares	■ newly issued shares or expansion of capital base ■ setting up a workers' ownership trust fund	mostly relevant for workers' cooperatives	Planned: Hungary and Lithuania
d) Management buy-ins (also leveraged)	- an individual or a group of individuals outside the firm buys the enterprise, but offers concrete restructuring programs, becoming the new management of the firm			Planned: Macedonia
6. Spontaneous privatization: ■ no state directives but initiated and carried out by enterprises themselves ■ state organizations active	■ found companies making use of state assets: - part of property turned into joint stock or limited liability companies - found individual companies with factories, plants, administrative	■ SOE continues operations with remaining assets ■ former enterprise left with the function of asset management ■ new owners: - managers and workers - banks	■ need competent and skilled management and stable work force ■ incentive productivity ■ unknown potential cash flow ■ overmanned/ minimize lay-offs ■ uncertain asset value	All countries

Method of privatization	Procedure	Options	Features	Use in transforming economies
	departments.	- other enterprises - foreign investors (limited)	■ assets undervalued	China, Latvia, All countries for trade and catering
7. Lease	■ right to use specified facilities for a fixed period of time ■ obligation to pay a fee to the owner	- temporary measure: intermediate phase before privatization, i.e., turning unprofitable into profitable venture before privatization	■ no transfer of ownership ■ no divestiture of assets ■ lessee assumes full commercial risk for operating the assets ■ lessee hires personnel	

8. Give-away schemes (also called mass privatization)	■ compensation vouchers/ownership certificates
	■ privatization cheques
	■ investment vouchers or coupons
	■ certificates of investment or ownership funds
		■ direct:
		  - to employees
		  - to public
		■ indirect: firms allocated to intermediaries
		■ free
		■ nominal fee
		■ on credit
		■ by installments
		■ transferable or not
			■ no revenue for the state
			■ in theory: rapid, equitable, not discretionary
				In progress: Czech Rep., Estonia, Kazakhstan, Lithuania, Romania, Russia, Slovak Rep., Ukraine
				
				Planned: Albania, Armenia, Belarus, Hungary, Latvia, Moldavia, Poland.

Source: Daviddi, R. (1995). pp. 12-14

Daviddi (1995, p. 16) claims that among the privatization techniques used, it is the mass privatization, which he calls the give away scheme,[47] that seems to have an advantage in the implementation in transforming economies in terms of speedy implementation without corruption. This is possible because the technique is non-discretionary and the rules are transparent. The other advantage is that the transfer of the resource can be implemented even if the local citizens do not have the capital to participate in the privatization process. The vouchers which are distributed to the general citizenry can be traded in the market. Thus any single individual with a relatively high interest on a certain asset could collect the vouchers by buying from other disinterested individuals. These vouchers can then be used to participate in bidding for some enterprises or specific assets. In the sense, it takes the form of money in a system without the necessary infrastructure for the financial institutions which would normally facilitate such activities.

In many of the transforming economies, a centralized office is in charge of the whole program.[48] Thus, even if mass privatization could be, as Daviddi claims, the most appropriate solution to the privatization problem of the transforming economies, the central agency in charge did not always adopt this scheme. In reality, the program is a mixture of different schemes, from bilateral negotiations, to public offering. In many cases, public offering is seen to be almost impossible to implement because of the absence of an appropriate market that will send the correct signal of the true prices of the assets or the enterprises being sold. Considering the problems attached to the whole problem of transformation, the high inflation rate has in fact discounted whatever savings the people have, thus making it also difficult to participate in the privatization via private and/or public offering.

In some countries, restitution is also adopted as a form of privatization. This is especially in cases where the ownership of the asset is clearly established. Remember that many of the large assets (such as land) and/or enterprises were confiscated by the socialist regime without due regard to the owners.

Lastly, auctions appear to have been also adopted, but mainly in small scale assets and enterprises; never in a big scale involving a group of assets.

---

[47] Give away because the government in effect does not gain any revenue from the privatization scheme.

[48] In the former GDR, this is the *Treuhand,* which existed until 1994.

2.4 Preliminary assessment of the results of privatization activities

As previously discussed, it will be difficult to make a definitive statement on the overall impact of the privatization activities in the transforming economies. Very little time has so far elapsed to allow one to make valid conclusions about the long-term effects in the privatizing economy. However, at this point in time, it is possible to make a general assessment on the status of the program, and the improvements as well as difficulties that the governments have experienced in the process.

Table 2.2 shows the status of the privatization program as well as the share of the private sector in the gross domestic product of selected transforming economies.

Table 2.2. Status of transformation of selected ex-socialist economies to market economy.

Country	Share of the Private Sector in GDP 1994	Privatization Large Firms	Small
Bulgaria	40	2	2
Estonia	55	3	4
Georgia	20	1	2
Lithuania	50	3	4
Moldavia	20	2	2
Poland	55	3	4
Romania	35	2	3
Russia	50	3	3
Slovak Rep	55	3	4
Czech Rep	65	4	4
Ukraine	30	1	2
Hungary	55	3	4

Note: 4 = market economy   1= small advance

Source: Aoki and Kim (1995) p. 20.

The highest achievement has been shown by the Czech Republic, a country that adopted the big bang process in transformation activities. Its private sector has the highest contribution to the country's GDP. The privatization activity has, already in the year 1994, been assessed to have achieved a status that puts the economy's private sector in a comparable level with that normally observed in a market economy. On the other hand, Hungary, Poland, and the Slovak Republic, all with the second highest share of the private sector contribution to the GDP, shows a good progress in privatization, although some work still needs to be done in the privatization of large enterprises.

In the whole, it may be observed from the table that there is a strong relationship between the rate of privatization of the state-owned assets and the contribution of the private sector to the countries' GDP. The slower is the progress in the transfer of the property rights, the lower is the rate of private sector contribution to the GDP, thus, still leaving the marks of the old regime with a huge public sector share. The problem is, if indeed the thesis is true that the public sector is grossly inefficient on account of the absence of incentives on the part of the managers as well as employees to perform well, then the inability to push the privatization program will mean a slow economic growth, or worse, stagnation coupled with other problems (like inflation, unemployment) that further aggravates the problem.

The assessment of the contribution of the private sector to the *growth* of the economies in transition may be more difficult to do because of the lack of statistics on this aspect. However, in most countries, the ratio of the increment in the output of the private sector to GDP (in current prices) was largely positive. Although this can be used as a positive indicator of the contribution of the private sector to the growth of the economy, it may largely be due to the mere transfer of the enterprises to private hands, but may or may not, in addition, speak of any increase in productivity as a result of the privatization.[49] Care should therefore be taken in the interpretation of the figures.

It is also essential to have in mind the consequences of a political signal to undertake privatization rather gradually over a longer period of time. The public sector in charge of the public enterprises will lose its long-term perspective in terms of a stable career in the enterprise when at some point in the future, the enterprise will anyway be transferred to private hands which will change the management structure. Nobody can claim job security. There is thus a danger, within the period of waiting, for an increased in corruption and ill activities within the enterprise. Even managers can enrich themselves, without facing too high a risk because the public at large has no

---

[49] Economic Commission for Europe (1995) p. 85. Surveys of a number of enterprises in various countries have shown that the private sector has exhibited the highest real growth rates, and this applies both on newly established firms as well as privatized firms. This also somehow supports the thesis that the private sector expansion is something positive for the economy.

residual interest in the enterprise. Being too careful in the privatization process can thus impose a high price to pay for the transforming economy.

So far, many of the privatization programs have led to a net loss for the state budget (Daviddi, 1995). This is perhaps attributable to the highly politicized nature of the privatization process, preventing the politicians from up front saying that the target is to increase revenue which then should be added to the budget pie. In theory, there should be a positive budget effect in the short run even if the assets/enterprises are not sold following the objectives of revenue maximization. By getting rid of state enterprises which are permanently on the red, the state releases the burden of inefficiency of its production activities, thereby releasing some money for other purposes. Table 2.3 presents the budget accounts of selected countries.

Table 2.3. Budget accounts of selected transforming economies, 1993-94. (in national currency and percent of GDP)

Countries	1993		1994	
	Amount	Percent GDP	Amount	Percent GDP
Bulgaria	-33.0	-11.5	-24.8	...
Estonia	32.0	1.4	453	...
Lithuania	9.3	0.8	-338	...
Moldavia	-13.7	-6.5	-0.189	...
Poland	-4.3	-2.8	-5.9	-2.8
Romania	-521.2	-2.6	-2,070.2	-4.3
Russia	-15.5	-9.8	-60.1	-10.4
Slovak Rep	-23.0	-6.8	-22.8	-5.7
Czech Rep	1.1	0.1	10.4	1.0
Ukraine	-7.6	-6.5	-109.0	-10.5
Hungary	-340	...	-322	-7.5

Source: Economic Commission for Europe (1995). p. 171.

Again, except for the Czech Republic (and Estonia), most countries ran budget deficits up to more than 10 percent of their GDP. In 1994, the budget surplus of the Czech Republic even reached 1.0 percent of the GDP, a dramatic increase from the previous year's 0.1 percent. The table, when read together with the previous table, shows the positive impact of the rate of privatization on the budget. Theoretically, such state revenues could have the potentials in pushing the economy faster towards development, via the investments in public goods. However, whether these finances were put to good use by the government, and whether the speedy privatization has also achieved efficiency to guarantee a stable long-term growth, cannot be established from the data.[50]

---

[50] Care should be taken on this matter, as there could be conflicts vis-a-vis the Keynesian economic principles., which indicate that a budget surplus can have a contractionary effect on the real sector. This research does not intend to discuss in detail the well-known incompatibility of the microeconomic theory (or the public finance literature) with the aggregate macro model of Keynesian economics, but it is important to recall that the efficiency of state expenditures is an irrelevant matter in the latter, mainly due to the disappearance of the micro activities in the process of aggregation.

Table 2.4 on the other hand shows how heavily the East German privatization program has been supported by the West Germans, making it possible to realize a speedy implementation of their transformation program, without due reference to the budgetary restrictions that has plagued the other transforming economies.

Table 2.4. Transfers from West Germany to East Germany. (in Billion DM), and budget deficit of the *Treuhand*.

	1991	1992	1993	1994	1995
Financial transfers from communal organizations	112.0	133.0	154.5	146.5	161.5
- German Unification Funds	35.0	36.0	36.5	36	
- Net transfers from the other states	66.0	85.0	106.5	99.5	113.5
- Sales tax and finance equalization	11.0	11.5	11.5	11.0	48.0
Financial transfers for Social Security	43.0	29.0	24.0	33.5	32.5
- Unemployment insurance	21.5	24.5	15.0	19.5	17.5
- Retirement insurance	21.5	4.5	9.0	14.0	15.0
Total public transfers	155.0	162.0	178.5	180.0	194
Budget Deficit of the THA	19.9	29.6	38.1	37.1	-

Source: Neubäumer, R. (1996). p. 580.

2.5 Issues in the privatization of land in transforming economies

The privatization of land in transforming economies is a difficult and complex activity which up to now is a subject of debates among the politicians in the countries involved. Although the basic idea is the same as in privatizing the other types of resources, the distinct characteristic of the resource land and the emotional attachment of the locals to its possession and ownership make it unique, thus requiring special attention in the design of the privatization program. Several points are hereunder discussed to highlight the issues that surround the activities towards the transfer of property rights to private individuals.

2.5.1 Farm restructuring.

It is widely known that the socialist regime has left a structure in agriculture characterized by large farms, either collective or state, which have farm sizes up to thousands of hectares. Although efforts have been exerted to transfer some of the land to private individuals via mechanisms such as restitution or voucher privatization (as in Russia where some land shares were distributed to the farmers actually tilling the land), such transfers are accompanied by complications. In the former, problems in adjudication of competing claims, identification of assets and boundaries, and the very simple but crucial registry of new owners seem to be common among most of the transforming economies (Brooks, 1993). This is a result of, among others, changes in the physical boundaries of the plots of lands which were confiscated during the old regime, because farms (especially the small ones) were restructured to fit into the large scale farming activities that was the standard practice in those times. The other problem that aggravates this is the fact that although the supply of land resources cannot be increased, the assets attached to it can. Through the years, it is apparent that farm assets have been added to the agricultural farms, making it difficult to identify who the rightful owner of these assets are. Separation of the land and other assets becomes a major problem, and thus a move towards another structure that might be preferred by the owner for one reason or another could not be accomplished.

Farmers who now recognize the totally new market environment see the problems in decision-making situations they face. For those restituted farms which are relatively small, it is widely observed that the farmers choose to stay with the collective. This allows the farmers to avoid the risk of being an independent farmer in the new environment. Most of these farmers rather prefer to continue to enjoy an employee status, than face the extreme uncertainty of being an independent farmer. The incentive to improve their efforts to be able to increase the total efficiency of the farms is simply lacking (Csaki and Lerman, 1996), and the old structures and governance system remain; the farms in most cases remain inefficient.

Privatization of land via the distribution of shares appears to be the quickest way to implement the transfer of property rights to private individuals, but again, it suffers from the problem of clearly identifying which particular unit of land is actually owned. Apart from the same problems this poses in terms of the lack of incentives of the worker-owners (e.g. in labor-managed firms), there are problems of defining the regulations of entry into and exit from the firm. There is no particular unit of land identified as legally owned by a certain farmer, and thus in cases of any wish to leave the firm, a farmer will face difficulties, if he wants to take with him his share. There is a greater incentive to stay in the farm because then he continues to gain as long as the farm is productive; there is no flexibility in case the farmer anyway decides otherwise. This also perpetuates the maintenance of the old structure, and thus coddles the continued inefficiency of the farm. Csaki and Lerman (1996, p. 213) cite that the fact that these labor-managed farms are not seen to be naturally occurring in the established market economies should be an indicator of its relative unsuitability in a market environment. The stumbling block that prevents the farms from developing to another form must be one issue that must not be left aside by planners.

To overcome such problems is a task that must be incorporated in the design of the privatization program. The program must not only consider the speedy transfer of the resource to private individuals, but it must take into consideration that the old system and its corresponding physical structures must be given the freedom to undertake the necessary adjustments. However, this is also very much related to the incentive structures attached ex-post transfer of the property rights. As long as the individuals do not have the right incentive to make the definitive move to change towards a more efficient and independent market-oriented activity, the old inefficient structure will prevail, and the agricultural sector faces the danger of stagnation.

2.5.2 Valuation of land and farm assets.

The old regime is characterized by the absence of a land market. Except for Poland, most of the farms in the ex-socialist economies were either belonging to the state or collective farms. Private farms which become part of the collectives are anyway not bought and sold. As a consequence, there is no established institution for determining the "correct" prices of these lands. The problem is aggravated by the fact that the farm assets also did not have the standard market value as is familiar in market economies. This contributes to the uncertainty in the valuation of the shares received from the government for the mass privatization of land. Using other countries with established markets as an example is not necessarily the best solution since the local conditions that determine the price are very much different.

Thus, how the correct prices are to be established should be one of the key areas that must be considered in the process of privatization. If the correct prices are established, the theoretical literature says that this leads to efficiency, both allocative and productive, and thus leads to improvements in welfare.

2.5.3 Parcelization, synergies, and economies of scale

One of the issues that has to be resolved in the design of the privatization process that is also related to farm restructuring is parcelization. This is obviously not a decision that requires looking only at the short term economic gains of the particular combinations of parcels that maximizes the profit of the farm, but rather looking into the long-term gains and stability of the structure of the farm as a business. This requires combined reflections on the synergetic effects of the parcelization, to take advantage of efficiency gains. This information will be difficult for the government to establish, as it is private information to the individual manager/owner, and the design of the optimal factor combinations will always vary across different types of individuals and production technologies. As will be shown later, the best that the privatizing government could do is to create an atmosphere of a free market for entry and exit in the land market, until the appropriate structure evolves. The individuals should be given a free hand to collect whatever information they need to design an appropriate management plan that will include decisions on combinations of various types of land as well as vertical/horizontal integration options in order to achieve efficiency. This is also incentive-compatible to the owners. Freedom in the decision towards the use and disposal of the land gives them the residual rights which will in general guarantee that the farms will be used to their optimum productive capacity, as long as there are no further barriers (physical, policy, or information) towards its achievement.

2.5.4 Political, institutional and legal problems.

One common feature of privatization among the transforming economies is the attempt to design the program that will solve some apparent social issues, making the whole issue of privatization highly political. This leads to frustration and the consequent delay in the reform process, and the agricultural sector is somehow taking the lead in this area. It is admittedly difficult for politicians to close their eyes on such social issues that beset the sector. However, too much focus on these social issues has rather led to the slow development of the agricultural market, because the main issues of the agricultural reform that targets efficiency based on private ownership is put aside. This can be verified via the widespread implementation of administrative procedures for privatization; on the one hand the government promotes private sector ownership, on the other hand it imposes too many legal and administrative restrictions on the decision towards the use and disposal of land that it is hardly correct to say that the land is *de facto* privately owned. In addition to being incentive-incompatible to efficiency, such administrative procedures are generally costly, and there is no apparent guarantee that the initial objectives of the government in the implementation process will be achieved, despite the high cost.

In some countries which require long periods of moratorium on the resale of purchased land, financial institutions will have no incentives to lend to the owners, simply because they will have no use for a collateral that is not salable in the market. Farm owners will then have no chance to survive if they choose to be independent, unless the government provides the needed capital to support their operations. This is again one of the problems that face the governments at the moment; too many businesses which are on soft budget constraints put pressure on the finances of the government, which drags the reform process, including the privatization of firms, especially banks. This, in the end is anyway shouldered by the average individual, who pays the price for the decisions of the government.

If it is the objective of the politicians to alleviate the social problems in the sector, they should rather take an active role in supporting the development and evolution of the agricultural farms toward more efficient structures. This will be sufficient to contribute to the solution of the existing social problems within the sector.

2.5.5 A case in point: East German land privatization

The East German privatization process is seen to be the most advanced among all the transforming economies. Apart from the support provided by the big brother, West Germany, the government actively pushed for a privatization program that is to be implemented at the shortest possible time. For the privatization of land, the main policy adopted was restitution wherever possible. However, there is still some total of 20 percent of the agricultural land that has to be privatized via mechanisms other than restitution. Such lands were the subject of soviet military confiscations in the year 1945-49. According to the *two-plus-four treaty*, these lands will be exempt from restitution. This legal background has been supported by the German *Bundesverfassungsgericht*, and even by the European Parliament. In the period following the reunification, it was the responsibility of the defunct *Treuhandanstalt* to privatize these lands, which total about 1.3 million hectares. However, due to political and other problems, the actual privatization has been postponed. Instead, most lands have been leased out, initially on contracts of 1-2 years, but now most are on long-term contracts for 12 years. After the *Treuhand*, the ownership of the land has been transferred to the *BvS*,[51] which has then assigned the *BVVG*[52] the legal rights to the ownership and management until these lands are finally privatized.

Although the original plan was to privatize as quick as possible, the reality proved to be more difficult. After long political discussions and several proposals on the appropriate way to implement the privatization program, the *EALG*[53] has been passed in 1994, giving a proper legal background for the implementation process. However, the *BVVG* has the final decision on the implementation *mechanism*.

Despite the fact that the announcements in offer-for-sale programs have started as early as in December 1995 in Germany, practically no sale has yet occurred in the state-owned land being administered by the *BVVG*. The heart of the process is the submission of a *management plan*, which is supposed to contain all the necessary information for investment, employment and other relevant production parameters that the interested bidder will use and employ if and when the land in question is won. The procedure adopted is an administrative one that is aimed at ensuring the "best" choice of the land owner, where the management concept submitted by the bidder is the most important basis for evaluation.[54] There is a base price by which the land must be paid, but this is not the critical factor in winning. It has been declared that the *quality* of the management plan submitted will be the deciding factor that will determine the winner. The price is secondary in the decision, and it becomes important only in case the

---

[51] *Bundesanstalt für vereinigungsbedingte Sonderaufgaben (BvS)*, the successor organization of the defunct Treuhandanstalt.

[52] *Boden Verwertungs- und Verwaltungsgesellschaft*, a limited liability company which now owns the state lands. It has taken over full responsibility for privatization from the *BvS*.

[53] Entschädigungs- und Ausgleichsleistungstungsgesetz.

[54] See Figure 2.1 for the illustration of the decision process involved in the German land sell-off program. It is the BVVG who will be responsible for evaluating these plans, but as the figure shows, will be done in coordination with other government, federal and national, institutions.

offered price is lower than the minimum price set by the *BVVG*. If this is the case, a good management plan will still be ranked first, and a sort of financial bargaining will be conducted with the bidder. That is, the candidate will be given a chance to reconsider his price offer. The process is also multi-stage in the sense that land units which are clearly identified and with no legal impediments are immediately put up for sale.

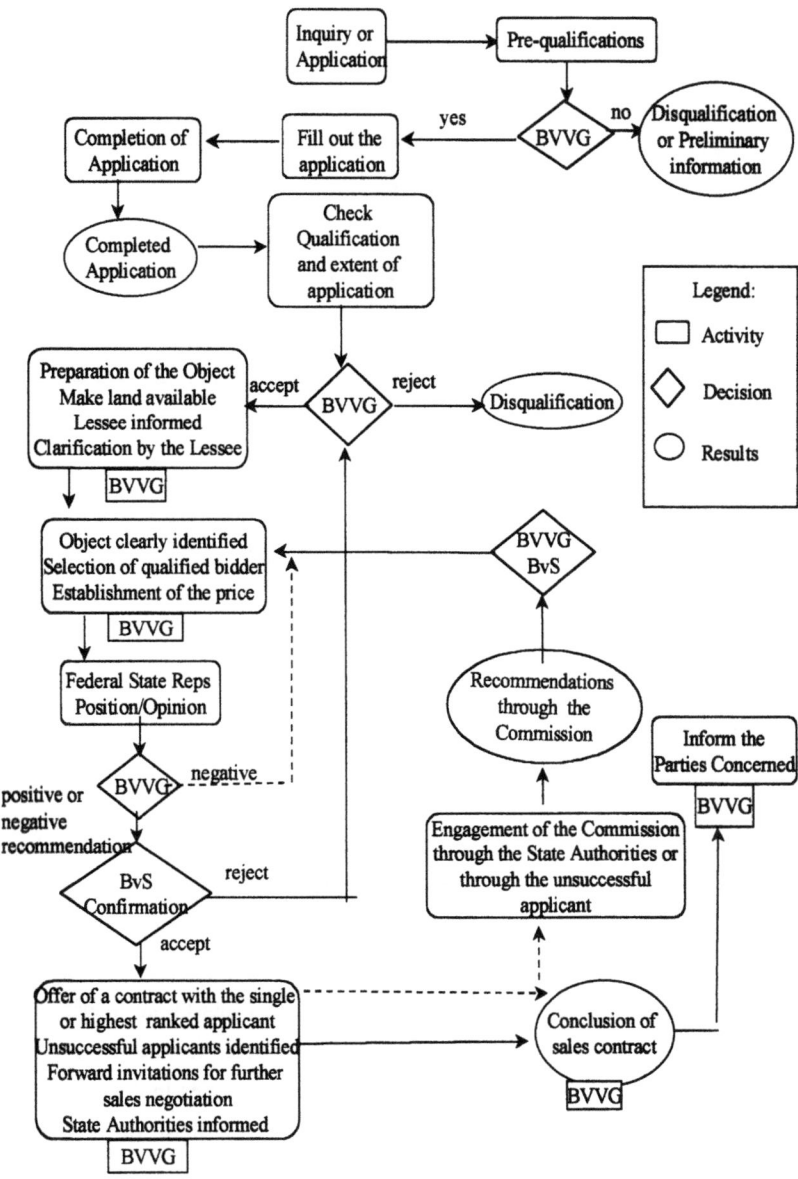

Figure 2.1. Schematic diagram of the BVVG process according to the EALG.

Source:Böhme, K. (1996) p.192.

2.5.6 Other transforming economies

The most recent data indicate a variability in the schemes implemented. Table 2.5 reveals that the degree of implementation of privatization is as variable as the schemes implemented across different transforming economies. It shows the current structure of privatized farms and its composition in the transforming economies.

Table 2.5. Share of private farms and their average size.

	% Share		Average size (ha)	
	pre-1990	current	pre-1990	current
Albania	3	88	-	1.4
Bulgaria	10	19	0.4	0.6
Czech Rep.	1	49	4.0	16.0
Slovak Rep.	6	13	0.3	1.0
Hungary	6	38	0.3	1.9
Poland	77	78	6.6	6.7
Romania	25	51	1.5	1.8
Estonia	5	67	0.5	2.1
Latvia	5	81	0.5	5.8
Lithuania	8	67	0.5	3.1

Source: Csaki and Lerman (1996) p. 222.

The table confirms that the task of land privatization in some countries has barely begun. In some countries, some progress has been made, but there is still a lot to be done even if the target is not 100 percent private ownership. Except for the Czech Republic, most countries have average farm sizes that are less than 10 ha. If the findings of the researches on privatization are correct, then this initial distribution of land as well as the farm sizes need to undergo some changes toward more efficient forms. That the countries have adopted various different strategies in the privatization process may be inferred from the data, and the reasons for these differences will likewise be as varied.

It has also been established that most of the countries have so far adopted very restrictive policies on the land transactions. Many have imposed limitations on the size of land that can be acquired, as well as moratoriums on the period by which the land is not allowed to be sold. This policy can also be seen in the more advanced East Germany. These impositions have been done largely due to the fear of *land concentration* in the hands of a few. There are certain instances when the ban is extended either for a long period of time (20 years in Germany) or indefinitely. Expropriation can also result from the inability to comply with the prescribed land use practices. In many cases, absentee farming is also avoided by imposing it outright. In East Germany, prospective owners of land must be either former owners or farmers who are living directly where the land in question is located.

3. Objectives and scope of the study

The objective of the research is to provide an analytic framework for the privatization of agricultural land in transforming economies using auction mechanisms. Although the reasons why this has been taken up as a major task of the research was already partly explained by the discussion in the previous chapters, this chapter will summarize the major arguments raised in the previous chapters, and in addition, will also provide an overview of what is to be expected in the rest of the paper.

One of the most striking predictions made is that the initial patterns of ownership resulting from any program of privatization are unlikely to be optimal (Gray, 1996).[55] If the outcome is indeed suboptimal, then the mere transfer of the resource to private hands is not the major task in privatization, but rather the parallel creation of a market that allows the private sector to make the necessary adjustment in the ownership structure which will eventually encourage the evolution of more efficient forms or patterns of ownership. This is only possible if, among others, the three basic rights cited earlier are guaranteed to result from the initial privatization activities, thus leading to a clearly defined transfer of property rights.

A closer examination of the problem in land privatization will lead one to conclude that the issues in this market are not unique if compared to the other sectors of the economy. The same political/ideological and economic principles apply to the process of transferring the ownership of agricultural land as well as the assets attached to it. The adoption of corrective measures to the confiscation of properties in the past by the socialist governments is considered as a politically important matter if constitutional and legal rights of the citizenry are to be respected. This is true in Germany, and the problem applies not only to the East Germans but as well to the West Germans. A number of West German citizens are actually former owners of the large agricultural estates confiscated by the socialist regime, and many, if not all of them, want their properties back.[56] Parallel to the adoption of corrective measures, the privatization process must also lead to the creation of efficient farm structures. In most countries,

---

[55] The reasons offered for this may be varied, but in general, it is hypothesized that this is the result of a poor design of the privatization process.

[56] The *Two-plus-Four Treaty* prevents restitution of about 1.3 million hectares of agricultural land confiscated during the soviet military rule.

this has been identified to be as important, and in Germany, is explicitly indicated in the *Treuhandgesetz*. Although results of high efficiency in resource use could be an important achievement, the experience suggests the reverse - - that the initial structure obtained directly after privatization is inefficient. This is consistent with what Gray (1996) has claimed. The institutional framework designed ex-post privatization thus becomes relatively important; it needs to be established whether the institutional mechanisms set up by the government allow adjustments to make it possible for the market to move toward more efficiency.

Csaki and Lerman (1996) cite that empirical evidence across various cultures and political regimes show that the most efficient form of agricultural production is based on secure and unrestricted private ownership of land and productive assets.[57] Csaki and Lerman extend this concept beyond mere efficiency to declare that any form of restriction in private ownership of the most productive agricultural asset, which is land, is *inequitable*. Security and unrestricted ownership should be considered as the preconditions of an effective agricultural transformation.[58] Productivity improvements in the land market due to unrestricted ownership should then also lead to improvements in the general welfare of both the producers and the consumers in the agricultural sector. Thus equity and efficiency in this sense are intertwined; providing the institutional mechanism for further market adjustments is efficient and equitable.

If it has been generally agreed upon among the transforming economies that privatization is indeed an important activity to undertake, the next major task of agricultural transformation is to move the market closer, if not directly to, the point of efficiency. There are two ways by which this can be done. One is to implement a rash transfer of property to private hands. In this case there is a greater need to address the post-privatization aspects, that is, to ensure that there is enough flexibility created in the market to allow the ownership of farms to change according to the principles of competition. The second one is to already target efficiency at the beginning; the task is therefore to select a mechanism of privatization whose outcome has properties of efficiency. For the longer term, mechanisms having both characteristics will be superior. The issue is not whether land should be privatized at all but rather, *how* it should be privatized. This research looks at the process of establishing a mechanism that moves the structure of resource ownership, at the first instance immediately after

---

[57] This is actually equivalent to the idea of full privatization proposed by Andreff (1992).

[58] not merely privatization.

54

privatization, to efficiency. Under which circumstances it can be achieved is an important result to be established.

In general, there is no single framework program to which these countries refer in order to design their programs.[59] Countries which are still to embark on a full scale privatization (such as Hungary, which has recently advertised an invitation for consultants in land privatization program design), have much to learn from the experiences of the others, such as from Albania, and partly from Germany.[60] Since data is scant to warrant a comprehensive empirical analysis of the experiences in land privatization, the focus of the research is on the analytical framework for an alternative auction mechanism.

3.1 Analytic Framework.

The analysis uses an information-theoretic approach. The privatization program is treated as a mechanism design problem where the government (the principal, or P) is seen to aim to make a contract (or sale) with the agents (A), and in the process also achieve certain objectives. Like many forms of P-A problems, the principal must take into consideration the incentives that the agents have to perform actions according to his (the principal's) wishes, in the presence of information asymmetry. But unlike the simple P-A problems, in agricultural land privatization, the value of the resource is not known with certainty, not by the seller, and not by the buyers. Land valuation is an issue which till now is a subject of research; the method of valuation is continuously evaluated and improved upon. At best, models are offered to approximate the price one should offer for land. Madden and Malcolm (1996), for instance, indicate that the final bid price for farm land, which is in some cases even critical to the survival of the farm family, are affected by many different factors, much more than that in non-land assets.

---

[59] Boycko, Schleifer, and Vishny (1996) offer a political economy approach to the analysis of the privatization problem, and Bös (1991) provides some analyses of the various aspects of privatization activities.

[60] However, Germany is currently facing problems in the course of the privatization of land. Apart from the enormous cost of the program to the government, there appears to be more land offered for ownership transfer than there are interested parties.

The modeling process undertaken in this research takes the idea of Madden and Malcolm into consideration.[61]

3.2 Mechanism Design and Auction.

The theory of mechanism design presupposes a principal whose aim is to maximize his expected utility subject to incentive compatibility (IC) and individual rationality (IR) constraints. In perfect information models where the "types" of the agents are known, the principal can always make a contract with the agent such that he gets the maximum rent out of the contract. In standard monopoly models, this is equivalent to selling each (divisible) unit of the good to the agent with the highest willingness to pay (WTP), and the IR for this consumer is thus binding (i.e., the consumer gets his reservation utility, and thus zero rent). In asymmetric information models where the agents possess private information on their willingness to pay (whether it is a certain or stochastic WTP), rent capture is not as easy, because the agent also wants to capture as much rent as possible from the resulting contract. This conflict of interest between the P and the A makes the mechanism of resource allocation difficult to design. In the face of information asymmetry, the best that the principal can do is to design an allocation mechanism (or in an auction mechanism, a payment function) where the accepted contract (IR constraint) also induces the agent to choose an action that is consistent with his own type, since this private information that affects the outcome is not available to the principal. In a selling mechanism developed by the principal, the action that the agent takes should be consistent with the IC constraint -- to offer a price that reflects his willingness to pay (say, high price for the type high WTP). The optimal contract in this condition of information asymmetry accommodates some inefficiencies; the equilibrium is characterized by a transfer of some of the risks from the (risk neutral) principal to the (risk averse) agent.[62]

It has also been established in the literature that ex-post efficiency is impossible to achieve in an environment where privacy of information is respected (Hurwicz, 1972).

---

[61] The reader is referred to the article of Samuelson (1990) for an interesting discussion on the price offered for land when there is serial correlation in the factors affecting the land price. This model shows what happens to land prices when say, a drought this year leading to a lower price this year could also increase the probability of a lower price in the following period. In this article, the author uses martingales to show that speculation in the face of negative autocorrelation in the sequence of price quotations does not give anyone a positive profit.

[62] The first best solution is to have the most risk tolerant individual, which is the principal, take all the risk.

Myerson and Satterthwaite (1983) have expanded this in the Bayesian-Nash environment of information asymmetry to say that it is not possible to have ex-post efficiency (i.e., that the IC constraints are satisfied with inequality[63]) and at the same time have voluntary participation, in which the rights of the agents towards the use of their information is respected. In their two-person bargaining model, they were able to show that if there is a positive probability of no trade (as in the case in the range of valuation when the seller's value exceeds that of the buyer), there is no ex-post efficient outcome. If ex-post efficiency is not guaranteed when IR is satisfied, the welfare implications of setting up a mechanism can be evaluated when a) the agents have not received their information on their types (*ex-ante*) ; and b) when the agents have received the information on their types but prior to sending off their messages (*interim*). The auction mechanism has been chosen among many forms of mechanisms for a number of reasons. One is that it has been established in the literature that auctions are an efficient solution to the P-A problem. Under certain circumstances, it can guarantee an efficient solution. Second, there has been recent experience in theory and practice that auctions can also be efficient in mass sales of public property. The experience of the auction of spectrum rights in the U.S. in late 1994, which has generated an unexpected government revenue of US$8 billion, has shown that the proper design of auctions through the help of theory can achieve the goals set in large-scale privatization programs (FCC Report (1993), McAfee and McMillan (1996) and Milgrom (1998), chapter 1.). The privatization involves the sale of the rights to use of the formerly military-owned radio and communications facilities. The spectrum rights sold represents the property rights on specific radio wavelengths used for wireless personal communication networks, such as those for beepers, handy, two way voice speakers, fax machines, etc. This sell off has some similarities with the sale of land on the basis of its use as an input to the production process. Radio spectra are also of various different qualities in different frequencies and wavelengths which could lead to quality differences in the final product produced. The spectra, apart from being distributed over different regions, can be combined in many different ways to form a specific quality and type of output. The returns to this asset is uncertain because it is dependent on the design of the technology , competition, and general economic conditions, among others.

---

[63] The formal definition will be presented in the next chapter.

Although many of the famous auction theorists were involved in the design process, the analyses employed were partial in nature, and no single unifying model was developed, partly because of the difficulty involved in the formal modeling of the complicated characteristics of the Bayesian-type environment of the auction. Two years after the spectrum sell off, a number of additional (partial analytic) models have been written by various authors explaining the various forms of possible equilibria, depending on the strengths of the main factors affecting the bidding environment.

Third, auctions are the most widely-seen institutional sell-off mechanism in the real world which has sound theoretical basis for implementation. Since the seminal paper of Vickrey[64] (1961), the theory has been consistently developed, but always as an explanation to what is observed in the real world, not the other way around, as one might usually expect. A well-known result in mechanism design literature is the existence of an infinite number of mechanisms that achieve the objective of the P. Theoretically, this is solved by the *revelation principle*, which has been proposed as a solution concept by Gibbard (1973), limiting the search to direct revelation mechanisms. To keep the balance between the theory and the actual problems to be dealt with in the privatization process, and to make the modeling process tractable, the auction mechanism design (which has an equivalent direct-revelation mechanism) is used as an analytical framework, keeping in mind the theory of mechanism design and the solution concept through the revelation principle. Fourth, from the legal definition of transfer of ownership and the achievement of efficiency, it was earlier argued that leasing schemes or any other semi-privatization measure will be short of the goals of both efficiency and equity, since these lack one of the three basic rights required in full privatization. From the point of view of the political ideology of democratic market economies, other forms of privatization in which the state retains some legal rights in use and disposal will be unacceptable. Full transfer is therefore the objective assumed in the analysis, and either direct transfers or a sell off is therefore called for. This research deals with the latter, the sell off, but tries to explore some given design considerations that could lead to the achievement of the goals of privatization, and to identify certain conflicts in the design and implementation, if it exists, so that appropriate policies can be guided in the process.

---

[64] He is one of the two awardees of the 1996 Nobel Prize in Economics for his contribution in the analysis of asymmetric information models, such as that in his 1961 pioneering paper on auction theory.

In the following two chapters, the theoretical background of the general mechanism design problem shall be discussed in more detail, followed by the specific concepts of auction mechanism design. A brief review of the applicability of this process in the market is done, and then the various modeling options for the problem in agricultural land privatization presented. Finally, the issues and implications regarding the use of auction as a solution to the problem of privatizing land are discussed in the last chapter.

4. The theory of incentives and mechanism design

Which of these systems is likely to be more efficient depends mainly on the question under which of them we can expect that fuller use will be made of existing knowledge.

F.A. von Hayek (1945)

In the previous chapters, the role of incentives and information has been discussed in various parts, hinting at the possible effects on the outcomes of any contracting situation, that is, including prices. Indirectly, the discussion was leading to the domain of the non-neo classical framework and the possible non-achievement of efficiency situations on account of information and incentive problems. The neo-classical framework presents a model where prices are assumed to be given, and as a result, the price system directs the allocation of resources to the point of efficiency. As F.A. Hayek (1945) has claimed, information is the single most important factor that drives the activities in the market. Thus, the prices that appear in the market contain all relevant information needed by the individuals in order to undertake efficient activities in the market. However, not all agents will be willing to accept the given prices; some will even dictate it (as in having an auctioneer). In real market situations, agents will have varying degrees of information, not only on prices, but on many other factors that may have an impact on the resulting contract. They will have various different "beliefs" which affect their decision-making activities. This chapter, as well as the following chapter, will address the theoretical background that surrounds the effect of information on bargaining between agents, and the role of information and beliefs in the outcome of the bargaining activity. The discussion starts with the bargaining situation from a game-theoretic framework. The aim is to provide a basic understanding of the incentives that drive the agents' decisions on the basis of information they have. The equilibrium conditions in information asymmetric models of bargaining will be characterized, to serve as a take off point for the following chapter on the theory of auctions. The privatization problem is again discussed in connection with the basic framework of mechanism design.

4.1 The nature of information

One of the most important determinants of the outcome of a game is the nature of information possessed by the participants of the game. The information structure can take many different forms, and the standard classification depends on the quality and quantity of information available to the players.

One classification is that of a game involving *perfect information*. It has the strongest requirement of all the types of information. All players posses every information relevant to the game and its outcome. This includes the strategies of the players, the payoffs of all the strategies and/or actions, and the actions taken so far. This game does not involve a simultaneous move of the players.[65] In addition, there is no move by nature before or after a player has taken an action.[66] This information structure provides the best conditions for formulating an optimal action on the part of the player.

A violation in any of the informational requirements in the structure of the perfect information game will of course change the information structure possessed by the players. This may lead to a change in the nature of the outcome of the game. Imagine a game involving simultaneous moves, but one knows all the possible strategies and actions that all the players can take. Simultaneity of moves results in uncertainty regarding the actions to be taken by the other player in the game. A player in this situation can only at best formulate an *expectation* of the most likely or best strategy of the others, given what they think his own best strategy is. This is the information used by the player to formulate his own best response. The information structure in this case becomes *imperfect*, indicating that the agent has all the necessary information other than the history of the game (or the moves made so far).

In another light, when all moves or actions of the players are directly observable, then the players are *certain* about what actions have so far been taken by all the players at any point in time. If nature moves after an action has been taken by any player [67], then all the other players will in general not know with certainty which action has been taken. Consequently, the information available to the players become *uncertain*. In this case the players can only form strategies based on the expectations of the outcomes,

---

[65] As simultaneity implies uncertainty as to the action to be taken by the other participants in the game.

[66] The outcome of a move of nature, when unknwon to at least one player, leads to uncertainty on the actions, types, of agents or outcomes.

[67] after which the state of nature is observable.

using their information on the probability of each of the states of the world, given an action to be taken.[68]

When players have *symmetric* information, then each one of them will have the same information structure, be it perfect, certain, or uncertain, at that time when the players have to make their moves. A situation where no one among the players knows anything can be an extreme example of a symmetric information structure. As soon as any single individual has information that is not available to the others, then the information structure is *asymmetric*.

If the information is *complete*, nature either does not make a move before the players make their action, or if there is a move by nature, this will be known or observable to the players.[69] Suppose that, before a player i (who knows his own type) makes a move, the types of the other players are known to be rather distributed over a possible range of values. The information structure is thus considered *incomplete*. If a player $i \neq j$ knows his type, but has, in addition, only the information about the possible valuations of all the others to be in the range of the same distribution, and that every $j \neq i$ is in the same situation, then the information structure is *symmetric* but *incomplete*. If everyone knows that everyone knows that everyone knows (*ad infinitum*) that the types are distributed over this range, then this information is considered to be *common knowledge*.

As a rough distinction of the equilibrium concepts between complete and incomplete information models, one can generally say that in the former, the equilibrium is referred to as *Nash* (in static games, and *sub-game perfect* in dynamic games with credible threats or promises), while in the latter, the equilibrium is referred to as *Bayesian-Nash*.[70]

Through most of the discussion and analyses in this research, the focus will be on the incomplete, asymmetric information models. In the mechanism design process representing the analysis of the solution of the principal-agent problem, there is initially an environment of information asymmetry between the principal and the agent(s). The latter have private information on their types that is relevant to the

---

[68] As one may notice, this incorporates notions of conditional probabilities.

[69] Thus, complete information can either be perfect or imperfect.

[70] As this research focuses on the latter, the reader is referred to basic game theory literature for a detailed discussion on complete information models and the Nash/sub-game perfect Nash concepts.

principal's objective in designing the mechanism. The principal, who has at best only the information on the possible distribution of the types of the agents, has to set up a mechanism or a game to be played by the agents in a way that maximizes his own objective function. The resulting equilibrium is a Bayesian-Nash equilibrium, which shall be discussed in more detail in the next chapter.

4.2 Information asymmetry and the P-A problem

Many economic decision-making situations involve principal-agent relationships. In this model, there is a *principal* who has to make a decision that is wholly or partly based on some information that he only knows imperfectly. This information is held as private information by the agents. The agents, in turn, have to make a decision on the basis of this private information, as well as on the general economic environment wherein the decisions have to be made. These decisions affect the well-being of the principal, through the effect of the actions on the outcome of the process.[71]

In this asymmetric information model, the task of the principal is to find ways and means to induce the agents to reveal the relevant information to him, as this will be critical to his utility maximization objective. There are various different ways to do this. One option to do this is to follow a dictatorship rule, whereby each agent is simply asked to reveal the information by law. Failure to comply could lead to punishment. In a democratic society, such a case is clearly not acceptable, and even if forced to be accepted, is extremely difficult to implement. One can argue that taxation is implemented in this manner; the state declares by law that everyone should reveal their incomes truthfully, which will then be used to calculate the income tax to be paid. If there will be no penalty for false declaration of taxes, almost everyone (except, say, those who are benevolent towards the socially weak who are the ones to benefit from the tax) will evade tax and declare zero incomes. However, as long as the expected value of the punishment is way below the expected value of returns from false declaration, there will always be a positive probability of evasion.[72] If private

---

[71] As a matter of comparison, imagine the classical monopoly situation. A monopolist, who has all the information about who the buyers are and their corresponding willingness to pay, will be able to extract all the rent from the sale. He can sell each (infinitely divisible) unit of the good to the buyer with the highest willingness to pay, thereby leaving each buyer with zero rent. If any single seller does not have this information, that is, that willingness to pay becomes private information, rent extraction becomes difficult.

[72] Note that the idea behind taxation is to raise the amount needed to finance the provision of a public good with inherent characteristics of free-riding.

information is respected because of the ideals of democracy, the government should rather set up an optimal tax scheme that is incentive-compatible to the revelation of the true income. Similarly, in public goods provision, this is equivalent to setting up a mechanism that gives an incentive to the beneficiaries to reveal their true willingness to pay for the public good to be provided.

The incentive compatibility of the voluntary information-revelation mechanism is one of the principal's major problems, and is the core of the analysis of the P-A problems. A truly acceptable and democratic incentive-compatible mechanism is one that respects the privacy of individuals' information (as a resource). It allows the individuals to determine the disposal of this resource on the basis of their own judgment and will.[73] Indeed, as discussed in chapter 2, this is an important aspect of privatization that has already been taken up as a political issue. In both large and small scale privatization programs, private information, just like any tangible asset, must be treated as a valuable resource that is part of the resource base owned by the individuals in the society. Private individuals should have the right and the freedom to decide on the use and disposal of their own resources. This is consistent with the notion of well-defined property rights in a democratic and just society.

There are many applications of the P-A model. These are, to name only a few, the cases of contract formation between employer and employee, insurance provision, sale of goods, corporate decision-making, and bank credit provision. An employee has private information on his labor efficiency, which is relevant to the determination of the efficiency wages. The seller has more information about the quality of the good than the buyer. The debtor has more information about the performance of his project financed by the bank. The insuree has better information about his health conditions than the insurer. The manager of the corporation has more information about the operations of the firm compared to the equity holders. These asymmetries often lead to situations that prevent efficient allocations from being achieved.[74] The inefficiency problems that arise from it vary depending on the nature of the information available to

---

[73] see chapter 2 for the arguments on acceptable privatization.

[74] Recall the fundamental welfare theorems in the Arrow-Debreu model, that the competitive equilibrium can be achieved and is Pareto-optimal, and that any Pareto allocation can be achieved as a competitive allocation given a redistribution of income of the agents. However, these are under the assumption that every agent in the economy possesses the same information as the others, i.e., in terms of prices etc., such that informational asymmetries do not exist. Or if not entirely symmetric, the market participants are able to observe the terms of the contract in the exchange, and thus any deal that they make already assumes that they have verified all the information and the act of making the contract shows that they agree to the terms, including the price.

the principal and the agent, as well as the timing of the existence of information asymmetry in relation to the decision-making of the principal and the agent. The various types of agency models under asymmetric information will be the topic to be discussed in the next section.

4.2.1 The Moral Hazard Problem

The moral hazard problem can be characterized by a situation whereby the information asymmetry arises *after* the principal has made a contract with an agent. In particular, it happens when a self-interested agent can perform actions that benefit him, but at the same time impose costs on the principal. By the very nature of the action taken by the agent, this move is not Pareto-efficient.[75] This inefficiency arises because the terms of the contract between the P and the A are such that the agent does not bear the full consequences led by his own actions. It is a problem *ex-post* contract, and it arises because either a) the action of the agent is not observable to the principal; or b) the action of the agent may be observable, but the information that he has which determined his action is not available to the principal. The first case is known as the *hidden action problem*, and the second case is the *hidden information problem*.[76] Both cases involve uncertainty in the information possessed by the principal regarding the action taken by the agent, or the information on the determinants of the action taken by the agent.

The standard literature on moral hazard with hidden action almost always starts with the discussion of the case of the employee-employer relationship, showing how the self-serving actions of the agents, after the contract is signed, can lead to the decrease of the principal's profits,[77] which in some cases could lead to a no-contract situation, if the employer has anticipated such actions before the contract is signed. This may be inefficient, especially if there are clear gains to the society in the formation of the contract. In the privatization process, one can refer to this model to explain

---

[75] Recall that a Pareto-efficient move is that which improves the utility of one without hurting any other.

[76] There are disagreements in the proper classification of the problem of hidden action and hidden information. Some would like to stick to the original definition of moral hazard, i.e., that which refers to the application in, say, car insurance when the insuree's actions, whether he is a careful driver or not, are not observable to the insurer. For the purpose of this research, a distinction is made, noting that both classifications are used as cases when moral hazard becomes a problem.

[77] Sometimes below the pre-contract levels.

privatization contracts which contain provisions on further actions that the agent should take after he has won the contract.[78]

Theoretically, the contract that can be agreed upon between the principal and the agent in general, depends on several things: a) the verifiability/separability of the agent's actions from the other's actions or other effects; b) degree of risk aversion of both the P and A; and c) observability of the state of the world.

When both the agent and the principal are risk-neutral, complete and enforceable contracts can be formed because the agent can be assigned the full residual rights or claims in return for a payment, that is, under the conditions that the agent's action can be distinguished from the others and that the state of the world is *observable*. In other words, in the case where the outcome is observable, and that the agents are risk neutral, a transfer payment can always be designed in such a way as to get the agent to choose the action that maximizes the principal's objective function. By assigning the residual rights to the agent, the principal can have an efficient outcome without having any loss for bearing risks. In most cases, it will be sufficient for the principal to guarantee a payment that is at least as good as the reservation utility of the agent. The solution is normally binding (i.e., the agent receives a payment that is equal to his reservation utility).

If the agent is risk averse, one expects that he will insure himself from any risky situation. In this case, the principal must provide some incentives for the agent to take some risks. This is done by establishing the minimum amount that the agent needs in order to achieve the outcome that the principal would like to have, and an additional

---

[78] This condition is actually to be observed in many privatization programs in the ex-socialist economies. The concern on the macroeconomic as well as other political and socio-economic factors in the transforming economies have led the privatizing institution to adopt additional "targets" in the course of the privatization process. These involve, among others, such contract clauses as employment and investment commitments, two of the most common factors of extreme interest to the policy-makers. Though these might have been formulated with the best of intentions, the policy-makers' failure to recognize the after-contract conditions that may lead to the adoptions of certain actions that are rather more incentive-compatible to the agent's interest than to the government often led to the poor performance of the privatized firms. The performance could be measured by the indicators of employment and investments actually made by the winning firm after winning the contract. Such conditions can, however, only be evaluated ex ante, but it is rather more efficient to look for policy tools or pre-contract mechanisms that will at least minimize the occurrence of such problems.

premium for risk. [79] In cases when the action is not entirely observable, there will be difficulty in buying full insurance cover against risks. These include the cases when the contract between the employer and the employee is based on the payment of a fixed wage based on his ex-ante productivity. Actual productivity may be difficult to verify because of a stochastic production level; the stochasticity is not only determined by the variability of the effort of the employee but also of other inputs in the production process. The effects of the agent's actions are mixed together with the effects of other variables to form the outcome, and an employer can observe the output but not the effort of the agent. The employee has the incentive to pretend to work too hard even in low levels of production. One possible solution to this is to design a payment scheme that has a fixed component, to take care of the reservation utility of the employee, and a variable component that is tied up with the level of production. In the farmer-landlord situation, the solution is to transfer the residual claims to the farmer by letting him pay a fixed rent for the land, and taking all the risks for the production activities. As long as the payment is acceptable to the landlord, and thus the contract is finalized with the farmer, the farmer will have the incentive to use his optimal effort. This is one of the standard results in the theory of tenancy. In privatization, the issue becomes more complicated. Targeting investment levels that are either partly or wholly determined by the actions and/or decisions taken by the owner-manager -- which affects the profitability of the firms -- leads to the same problem, even if the production levels and the actions are directly observable.

The problem of moral hazard with hidden information post-contract is attributable to the difference in information between the principal and the agent, but now this asymmetry takes another form. In many models of moral hazard with hidden information, the action is fully observable. However, the agent will have the private information on the factors that affect his choice of actions, which again, affects the

---

[79] An example is the contract between the farmer and the landlord. The farmer has a disutility for work, and a utility for his share of income from production. In this case, the landlord who is the principal, must be able to design a sharing arrangement that guarantees the reservation utility of the farmer, generated by the lowest possible effort the farmer will exert to keep the contract, plus an additional margin for taking risks, because production level is uncertain ex-ante. In any case, production is observable, and so the sharing can be determined with 100 percent certainty, unless the farmer misreports. In the latter case, the landlord cannot observe the actual output and is again subject to another type of moral hazard.

outcome of the contract. Again, such situations lead to a breakdown of the contract, whenever the principal fully anticipates such a condition.[80]

4.2.2 The Adverse Selection Problem

Unlike the moral hazard problem, the adverse selection problem arises *before* the contract is made between the principal and the agent. The information asymmetry arises as a pre-contractual condition; the principal is faced with a number of agents whose types are unknown to him. The types of the agents, which are private information, determine the action to be taken by the agents, which in turn determine outcome of the contract. Self-serving agents will have the incentive to lie about their types if there will be a gain in doing so. In terms of the structure of information discussed in section 4.1, nature moves first; this is observed by the agents but not by the principal; the principal makes an offer of contract, and then the agents choose their actions which are self-serving. Akerlof (1970) pioneered the analysis of the situation of adverse selection in the market for lemons in the used car markets. In this article, he was able to show that if the problem of adverse selection exists, the equilibrium will be characterized by a situation whereby only lemons will be sold, which then leads to a market breakdown.[81]

There are other forms of P-A problems that are discussed in the literature. These are screening and self-selection problems. This author's point of view is that these are rather mechanisms that could possibly solve the adverse selection problem faced by the principal. In screening, the principal invests in the collection of some relevant

---

[80] An example of a P-A relationship in this model is between the shareholders of a company and its president or general manager. The president will in general know his utility given various different levels or types of effort. He will know whether or not he has a positive utility in undertaking a certain task. In standard contracting models, effort is always assumed to provide a negative utility to the individual. But there are indeed tasks where this assumption does not apply, and the principal will not know this. There are also certain investment decisions which the president can make which gives him relatively more utility than any other investment, and the shareholders will not know this. Another dimension of modeling involves a state-dependent utility function of the president, where the state of nature is observable only by the president. Thus, nature moves after the contract has been made; the agent observes this and then makes his action. The agent has an incentive to lie about reporting the state of nature if he has something to gain from it. This leads to inefficiency.

[81] This problem is often to be seen in the insurance market. An insuree will generally know whether he is a high risk-type, and therefore costing more to the P, or a low risk type, which costs less to the P. From the point of view of the P, it is better to have more of the latter, but the former will always have an incentive to declare that they are of the low-risk type, if this means paying a lower premium. Setting the right premium to separate the high risk from the low-risk is the central problem of the insurer. Otherwise, his inability to distinguish the types of insurees will impose costs on him that might also mean that offering no insurance will be better.

information on the types of the agents. The collected information need not be perfect. The idea is that in the process, the additional information should improve his expected payoff. He then has to compare the gains from the collection of the imperfect information to the cost. A positive net gain should encourage him to screen. Signaling, on the other hand, involves an investment on the part of the agent to collect some "signals" on his type that will be imperfectly observable to the principal. An example of a signal on the quality of a job applicant will be education. In both models, the information of the principal is improved, but the difference lies only on who makes the initial investment to solve the problems created by the information asymmetry.

4.2.3 The role of incentives

The principal-agent problems presented above are of course not without solutions. In general, the problems created by the informational asymmetries can be dealt with by looking at the incentives of the agents to undertake certain actions. It is generally to be observed that efficient contracts may not be formed when some factors of interest to the contracting parties are not observable. In the case of the moral hazard problem, although the action (or any information leading to the action) is not observable, it may be possible to use a proxy variable, say, output, to give an indirect information about the effort exerted by the agent.[82] In the adverse selection problem, the principal adopts a similar scheme, but that which already separates the individual types in the choice of a contract with the principal. In both of these P-A problems, the solution involves finding the efficient incentive contract that reveals indirectly the type of the agent. Unfortunately, there are of course some efficiency losses in the sense that the risk is shared between the risk-neutral principal and the risk-averse agent. However, a contract is formed that in the end raises the utility of both on the average, and this is favorable to the society in general.

The theoretical treatment of this modeling process is embodied in the theory of mechanism design. In general, the principal will have to look for ways to encourage the agents to accept a contract and at the same time have an incentive to reveal the

---

[82] The literature adds some regularity assumptions to this, of course. For instance, in a standard moral hazard with hidden action problem, the probability of getting a high output is higher when then the effort is high than when the effort is low. Similarly, the probability of getting a lower output is lower when the effort is high than when the effort is low. In this case, the principal can take the output as an indirect indicator of the effort level, and contracting can be done on the basis of the observable output. The information is of course imperfect, but it is better than having no information to base the contract on.

information that he is interested in. This he takes as a constraint in his expected utility maximization.

The next section discusses the framework in general terms. Chapter 5 continues with the application on auction mechanism design.

4.3 The Theory of Mechanism Design

Myerson (1989) defines a *mechanism* as a specification of how economic decisions are determined as a function of information that is held by individuals. Following this, the term mechanism shall be used interchangeably with an economic mechanism to refer to an institution that induces a certain direction in the actions to be taken by the participants in the mechanism. Fudenberg and Tirole (1991) provides a game-theoretic characterization of the mechanism design process to compose of three steps, viz.:

1. The principal designs a mechanism M, a contract or incentive scheme.
2. The agents simultaneously accept/reject M.
3. Agents who accept M play the game in M.

In step (1), the mechanism M has several components, but it mainly comprises a) the set of rules that defines how the agents will send their messages; and b) the corresponding allocation given the messages sent. Assume for discussion purposes that the message is the willingness to pay (WTP) in an economic mechanism called auction. The message can be sent in many different ways. The mechanism defines that everybody must gather in one place at the same time.[83] All announcements of the WTP will be made in public, and an auctioneer invites announcements of these messages every time an item is to be given out for sale. For each item, the messages, or the "bids" will be increased by an amount ε, until only one standing bid remains and there are no more bids offered. The allocation rule defines that the highest standing WTP, with no further offers, will allow the bidder to own the item. In other words, the ownership is transferred to that bidder who pays the highest among those gathered together to bid.

---

[83] This is the English auction. More on this in the next chapter.

In step (2), which is also called the individual rationality (IR) constraint[84], the agents who reject the game will be guaranteed a minimum utility, which is already pre-specified in the M. This means that participation is on the basis of free will. No one is forced to play this auction game. Anybody who is present in the hall expresses his acceptance of the rules set up in the M. This also means that, in joining the activity, each one expects to at least be as well off as before.

In step (3), the agents play the game, but acceptance does not guarantee incentive compatibility, that is, playing the game does not require nor guarantee that WTPs are revealed truthfully.[85]

Formally, a general mechanism M *contains*:

a) a message space μ_i for each of the agents $i = 1,....n$ with types $z = (z_1, z_2, ..., z_n)$, $z \in Z$ with a corresponding probability distribution $F(z)$ defined over its support $(\underline{z}, \overline{z})$ and utility function $u_i\ (y, z)$ that is of the von Neumann- Morgenstern type;

b) an accepted game form to announce message $\mu_i = (\mu_1, ... \mu_n)$;

c) an allocation rule $y\ \{q, t\} \Rightarrow y\ \{q(z), t\}$, dependent on type, where $q \in Q$ is the decision (say, to buy or not) and t are transfers from the principal to the agent.

In other words, the message is transmitted to form an allocation y via the mechanism

(1) $\quad y_M : \mu \rightarrow Y = \mathbf{Q} \times \mathbf{R}^n \qquad q \in \mathbf{Q}$

Assume for simplicity that the game involves direct revelation of types z. The objective of the principal is to find an allocation $y = \{q, t\}$ that maximizes his expected utility:

(2) $\quad U_0(z) = E_z u_0(y(z), z)$

---

[84] This term is used interchangeably with participation constraint, p.c. for short.

[85] In the auction game above, assume that a bidder's standing offer is 0.5 million DM, the highest so far, and there are no further tenders. Even if his true WTP is 1.0 million DM, he does not have to reveal this. Doing so reduces the rent available to him if he in fact wins. But still, even if he does not reveal his actual WTP, he revealed the information that he has the highest WTP.

where $i = 0$ refers to the index of the principal. The utility of the principal depends on the allocation mechanism y, which is in turn dependent on all the possible types, which is also the message z sent by the individuals.

The agent, on the other hand, maximizes the expected utility:[86]

$$(3) \quad U_i(z_i) = E_{z_{-i}}\left[u_i(y(z_i, z_{-i}), z_i, z_{-i}) | z_i\right]$$

The first argument of the agent's utility function is the allocation mechanism y, which is a function not only of his own type z_i (which could be a private information), but also of the types of the others z_{-i} (which is imperfectly known by i). In addition, the utility function is affected directly by the message that he sends, which is his own type, as well as the messages sent by the others on their corresponding types.[87] The expectation is taken across the types of the others, that is, excluding i, and is therefore represented as $-i$, conditional on the private information.[88]

4.3.1 Informationally decentralized mechanisms: existence and uniqueness

In the general mechanism described earlier, the EU maximizing principal sets up a mechanism that is acceptable to the agents. This is the same as saying that the mechanism defined by the rules of sending the messages and allocation satisfies the IR constraint.[89] The problem, according to Hurwicz (1972), is that there are infinite mechanisms available that will solve the problem of the P if the only constraint to consider is the IR constraint. More strongly, Hurwicz's *(Impossibility) theorem* states that in an environment with a *finite number of agents* which is also *informationally*

---

[86] Note that as in auction of contracts, where the principal pays the A to provide the goods and services,

$\frac{\partial u_i}{\partial t} = \frac{\partial u_i}{\partial y} \cdot \frac{\partial y}{\partial t} \geq 0$ for all $i \neq 0$ and $\frac{\partial u_0}{\partial t} < 0$. The agent receives money from the principal. In the case of sell

off, $t < 0$; the agent pays the principal, in return for the goods and services.

[87] Remember that the agents are free to decide on whether to tell the truth or to lie. Truth revelation will be discussed later. In general, his message will depend on what he expects the others to send as their message. His utility will depend on the message of the others, since the collection of all the messages will determine what the outcome is.

[88] To understand this, it is perhaps helpful to refer to an auction mechanism, where the probability of winning depends on the belief of the agent i on the valuation (type) of the others, $-i$, given his private information on his own valuation.

[89] Or the participation constraint.

decentralized, it is impossible to find a Pareto allocation in a Walrasian environment that is also *incentive-compatible*.[90]   To understand the impossibility theorem, a reference to the mechanism M and its constraints may be helpful. In step (2) of the mechanism design game, it was said that the agents simultaneously accept or reject the M. This is the same as what Hurwicz referred to as an informationally decentralized environment, where the agents have the option of participating (to accept M) or to refrain from participating (to reject M). This information decentralization is called the *no-trade* option. Those who choose to accept M have already evaluated M to be beneficial ex-ante; that they will be guaranteed their minimum utility on the average. Informational decentralization thus respects the privacy of the agents' information, and is central to a democratic type of economic institution.

The theorem has indeed quite pessimistic implications, since it is tantamount to saying that no economic institutional design can have the most important characteristic that has kept planners busy in targeting their policies: decentralization and efficiency. Later works have addressed this problem. One approach to the analysis is to find out the validity of this theorem under some other behavioral assumptions, as those normally to be observed in Nash equilibrium analysis. Under the Nash[91] environment, it has been proven that the theorem does not apply, since it was shown that (Pareto) efficiency *exists* in an environment with a no-trade option. However, even though it was shown to exist, it was also proven that it is *not unique*, and the problem is not really solved.

In later works, the Bayesian-Nash model was introduced as a refinement.[92] However, like the Hurwicz's theorem, it was shown that it is also impossible to find an equilibrium which respects the privacy of information in the sense of the no-trade option, with incentive compatibility.[93] The other problem relates to the inefficiency of the outcome in an environment of incomplete information, such as the case when the IR is binding, where all players get the reservation utility. In a bargaining game, this leads to a no-trade situation for *all* agents.[94] A proposed solution to this problem was

---

[90] see also Hurwicz, L. (1977) p. 425 ff.

[91] Assuming a behavior under the Nash environment is a refinement of the Hurwicz analysis because it considers the strategic behavior of the agents.

[92] Again, the Bayesian-Nash environment is a refinement because, unlike in the previous Nash environment, the analysis does not assume complete information.

[93] see Milgrom and Roberts (1992) p. 100 ff.

[94] This has been discussed in various other sources such as in Myerson and Satterthwaite (1983).

put forward by Gibbard (1973), through the application of what now is known to be the *Revelation Principle.*[95] Roughly, this principle says that one can simply confine the search to *acceptable mechanisms* (in step 2) in which the dominant strategy is to *directly reveal truthfully the information* on their types. To be implementable, there are two basic constraints that a mechanism M must satisfy to achieve the highest expected payoff in a Bayesian game: the IR constraint, and the incentive-compatibility constraint (IC), together with additional assumptions that guarantee the existence of this optimal M in a Bayesian-Nash equilibrium context. Simply put, one searches for the mechanism that already has the truth-telling equilibrium *and* the no-trade option for the players.[96]

4.3.2 The Revelation principle and the Myerson-Satterthwaite theorem.

One of the most important points advanced in the theory of mechanism design is the idea that in an environment of incomplete information, the principal has a gamut of different mechanisms to choose from, which all will lead to the achievement of his objective. He need not maximize his expected utility within the framework of a given mechanism that has been adopted for whatever reasons, say due to historical reasons. He need not stick to this specific mechanism because there could be other mechanisms that might be superior (or equivalently, more efficient) to this existing mechanism in terms of having an allocation that gives him a higher utility. The main problem faced, however, is to find the mechanism that is *incentive-compatible* to truthful revelation of the agents' private information, in case the agents agree to play the game specified in the mechanism.

Myerson (1989) have expanded the argument of information decentralization of Hurwicz to say that incentive constraints to *voluntary truthful revelation* should be viewed with equal importance as any resource constraint. Like the amount of resources available, the amount and quality of information can directly affect the outcome of the process induced or prescribed by the mechanism. As no rational individual will give away this private information unless it is also to his best interest, the core problem

---

[95] the concept will be discussed more formally in the next section.

[96] On the basis of this modeling technique, most if not all forms of markets or economic institutions and organizations can be seen as a mechanism.

addressed is practically the incentive compatibility of the action of the agent with respect to the principal's objective of utility maximization.

The "P-A problem" can, in the light of the discussion, be interchanged with the "mechanism design problem". In every situation requiring the principal to design a "contract" or an "institutional set-up" to make the agents respond according to his (the principal's) wishes, he must always consider the strategic behavior of the latter in the process of the design of the "terms of the contract" or the "rules of the game". The principal's main objective is to set-up a mechanism that maximizes his expected utility, on the basis of the incomplete information that he has about the actions that the agents will take. The private information of the agents on their types is the key to the solution of the principal's problem, and is also central to the concept of the revelation principle.

The revelation principle has a very important role in the determination of equilibrium mechanisms in a Bayesian-Nash environment. Apart from the desirability of the solution concept in an incomplete information model, the Bayesian-Nash equilibrium is also of interest because it provides a weaker notion of equilibrium compared to, say, the stronger dominant strategy equilibrium. In a Bayesian environment, the individuals are only required to have a strategy that *on the average* will fare well given that the others also use their equilibrium strategies. It thus subsumes the stricter dominant strategy equilibrium which requires desirability of a given strategy over all possible types of the other agents.

A definition of the revelation principle clarifies the idea behind the process:

> *The principle holding that any outcome that can be achieved by some mechanism under self-interested strategic behavior that is induced by the mechanism can also be achieved by a mechanism employing an honest mediator to whom the parties willingly report truthfully and who then implements the outcome that would have resulted from the original mechanism.* [97]

The central theme is that *any given equilibrium in a general mechanism* will have an equivalent *incentive-compatible mechanism* in which the dominant strategy is to reveal the true preferences. The role of the mediator is to essentially collect the private

---

[97] Milgrom and Roberts (1992), p. 603.

information and to recommend strategies to the agents that will achieve a certain outcome.[98] The agents are assumed to always obey the recommendations of the mediator.

4.3.3 Problems in equilibrium: ex-post, ex-ante, and interim equilibrium concepts.

In this section, the various types of equilibria will be presented to give a clear view of the differences on the basis of the available information and the character of the efficiency. Specifically, a distinction is made between the ex-post, ex-ante and interim equilibrium, which shall be defined formally.

A function which assigns a collective choice g $(z_1, ..., z_n)$ to the mapping of all possible types $Z \Rightarrow Q$ is *ex post* efficient if the allocation rule defined by $y\{q, t\}$ is such that the good is always allocated to the agent who has the highest possible valuation. In addition, it is informationally efficient, following Hurwicz's criterion.[99]

Thus, a mechanism M is a specification of the rules to make the *collective choice* that will lead to an outcome $y\{q, t\}$. The next task is to specify which mechanisms M would be able to *implement* the choice function in a Bayesian setting. Specifically, the interest is in a mechanism that *truthfully implements* the choice function, which is at the same time *ex post efficient*, because the resources should be allocated to the agent with the highest valuation. Such is consistent with the Paretian efficiency principles.

A mechanism M is said to be *truthfully implementable* (in the sense of Bayesian-Nash equilibrium) if for all $i = 1,...n$, and $z \in Z$,

(4) $\quad E_{z_{-i}}\left[u_i(g(z_i, z_{-i}), z_i)\middle| z_i\right] \geq E_{z_{-i}}\left[u_i(g(\hat{z}_i, z_{-i}), z_i)\middle| z_i\right]$

where $\hat{z}_i$ is any message other than the true type z_i.

---

[98] One can imagine the mediator to be an expert consultant in this case, who will know what strategy will be good for the agent to use, given the information that he has. However, the consultant should not reveal more information than the strategy that the agent i is supposed to use. In other words, each agent i will only have his information on the equilibrium strategy he should use, and nothing about the rest of the participants in the mechanism. This way, the privacy of the information is maintained, and informational biases do not arise as a result of the mediator's actions.

[99] the Hurwicz criterion is a standard measure for checking the efficiency of a plan or a mechanism.

which is simply the *incentive compatibility constraint* in a direct revelation game where the message $\mu = z$.[100]   The direct revelation mechanism can be written as $M = (Z_1,...Z_n, g(\cdot))$. Indeed, if such a direct revelation mechanism *exists* in a Bayesian-Nash equilibrium (with IC constraint), then the mechanism M is truthfully implementable.[101]

The existence of such an equilibrium in a Bayesian-Nash sense *guarantees* that the revelations would be truthful. In this case, the mechanism M is also ex-post efficient, because when types are revealed truthfully, the allocation is guaranteed to favor the one with the highest valuation.

As discussed earlier, it is also important to have a mechanism that is not in a form of dictatorship. Thus, implementable mechanisms must also be voluntary, i.e., that the mechanism satisfies an individual rationality constraint in which an agent may decide a no-trade option if it is in his best interest to do so. However, according to Myerson-Satterthwaite (1983), it is not possible to have ex-post efficiency (i.e., that the IC constraints are satisfied) and have voluntary participation, in which the rights of the agents towards the use of their information is respected. In their two-person bargaining model, they were able to show that if there is a positive probability that there is no trade (as in the case in the range of valuation when the seller's value exceeds that of the buyer), there is no ex-post efficient outcome.

If ex-post efficiency is not guaranteed when the IR is satisfied, it is still important to evaluate the welfare implications of setting up a mechanism M when a) the agents have not received their information on their types (*ex-ante*) ; and b) when the agents have received the information on their types but prior to sending off their messages (*interim*). After all, since the mechanism design is done before all the private information are revealed, it is also important to be able to compare various mechanisms on the basis of the information that is available at the time of the design. The implications of such is discussed in the following section.

A choice function $g(\cdot)$ implemented by M is *ex-ante* efficient if there is no other $\hat{g}(\cdot) \in G$ that gives at least his utility such that

---

[100] the informational incentive constraints are sometimes referred to as adverse selection constraints because it could also be seen as a representation of the problem of adverse selection problem. See Myerson (1989).

[101] see Fudenberg and Tirole (1991).

(5) $\quad E_{z_i}\left(u_i\left(z_i|\hat{g}\right)\right) \geq E_{z_i}\left(u_i\left(z_i|g\right)\right)$ for all $i = 1,...n$

and

(6) $\quad E_{z_i}\left(u_i\left(z_i|\hat{g}\right)\right) > E_{z_i}\left(u_i\left(z_i|g\right)\right)$ for some i.

As in the Pareto sense, nobody can be made better off in any other mechanism without anybody else being worse off, that is, at the time that the information on the types is not available to anyone; $g(\cdot)$ is the choice function that maximizes the utility of the individuals *on the average*, across all possible types that can be taken.

On the other hand, $g(\cdot)$ implemented in M is *interim efficient* if there is no $\hat{g} \in G$ such that, conditional on knowing his type $z_i \in Z$,

(7) $\quad u_i\left(z_i|\hat{g}\right) \geq u_i\left(z_i|g\right)$, for all types in Z and all $i = 1,...n$;

and

(8) $\quad u_i\left(z_i|\hat{g}\right) > u_i\left(z_i|g\right)$ for some i.

Again, nobody can do better in another mechanism without making at least one other agent worse off. If the individual i has the information on his own type, he knows that he will be better off in $g(\cdot)$.

Both notions of efficiency refers to a choice function that is *truthfully implementable*. The difference lies only on the *timing* of the receipt of private information. In the first, information is not yet available such that the maximization of the agent's utility is done over all possible types that i can take. In the second, apart from the known choice function $g(\cdot)$, private information on the type of the individual is also known *before* making the decision, which should in turn change the decision profile of the agent compared to the ex-ante notion. In particular, the agent should maximize his utility *conditional* on the private information that he has, and conditional on the possible range of types that the other agents can take in the game. Note that any i knows only the distribution of the types. One can also verify that the ex-ante notion of efficiency is a stronger form of efficiency than the interim efficiency. It is immediate that a choice function that is ex-ante efficient is also interim efficient. The next chapter applies the mechanism design concept to the auction design problem with many agents with a self-interested seller.[102]

4.3.4 Privatization Mechanism and the P-A problem

The interest of this research in P-A models rests on its usefulness in addressing the main problems faced in the privatization process. Many privatization problems can be characterized by a mixture of the various P-A problems. A state selling out companies or resources to the general public may be faced with the problem of adverse selection if it wants to award the firm/resource to the person who can manage it more efficiently. Individuals, juridical or natural, will have private information about their own managerial capabilities and therefore their ability to manage the resource efficiently. If revealing this information will give them a disadvantage in the privatization process, they will have the incentive to lie about their own types. Moral hazard problems can also arise if the transfer of property rights through the privatization involves some terms in the contract which are not incentive-compatible to the utility maximization objective of the agents ex-post contract. Examples could be in the use of the resource such as land in the production process; the winning individuals may employ some practices which may be environmentally destructive, because this provides them with the highest returns possible. From the point of view of the society, this may very well lead to net reductions in the social welfare, a complete turn around of the ex ante objectives of the privatizing government.

The inability of the government to take into consideration the potential problems of moral hazard and adverse selection may be the reason(s) for the poor performance of many of the privatized industries/resources in transforming economies. Even if the government has been fully aware of these problems, in some cases, the focus on the other "social" and "political" problems facing the decision-makers could override or even mask the negative results of pushing the P-A problems to the side.

To sum, this section has presented the theoretical framework of the generalized P-A problem. It has been shown that the results are largely determined by the information structure possessed by both the P and the A. In the face of information asymmetry, the

---

[102] A distinction is made because one can also postulate a benevolent seller who maximizes the total expected welfare of the agents. The term "self-interested" is used for a seller whose objective is to maximize his own expected utility, which in auction models with a risk-neutral P is also the revenue maximization.

task is to set up a mechanism where an agent will send "messages" to the P regarding the relevant information of interest. To set up this mechanism, the P must design the rules governing what the messages are and how these are to be sent: if the agents agree to participate, the P has, in addition, to consider a message transfer and allocation rule that makes the A better off on the average.

5. Auction mechanisms

The institution of auction that is to be seen in the modern times has roots that date back thousands of years ago. In the modern-day times, it is familiar to almost everybody that valuable pieces of artworks are mostly sold off at auction houses. The reasons are not too obvious, but some argue that this practice follows not only a tradition; it has some economic logic behind it, that is why it has remained as a solid "market" institution. One argument is that artworks have no known fixed price in the market; each artwork is unique from all the rest, and its price is thus unknown to the seller. The price is largely determined by the purely subjective evaluation of the individual who derives some pleasure in its ownership. Such private information is clearly difficult to collect, and even if subjective appreciation levels are available to the seller, it has to be translated to a common index of price or willingness to pay.

Christie's and Sotheby's, England's most popular auction houses, have established a major business of selling priced items via the most known auction form called the *English auction*. This type of auction commences in two ways; either (a) the auctioneer announces the reservation price, or b) the auctioneer calls for the first bid. After the first bid, calls for higher bids are invited, each with a specific increment say ε for every call. Each player is, at all points in time, informed of the current highest bid. The bid thus successively increases as each bidder tries to outbid the other, until eventually only one of them remains. The bids are always confirmed by the auctioneer, and the bidders commit themselves publicly, thus also the name *open auction*. Each player has an equal chance to renew his bid once he is outbidden. A bidder wins when no further (higher) tenders are offered. He pays a price equal to his current bid. This mechanism has a dynamic form, since agents continue to bid and re-bid until only one stays in the game.

The other popular auction can be traced back in the Netherlands, and thus the name *Dutch auction*. In contrast to the English auction, this mechanism follows a descending bidding procedure. It starts with the announcement of the highest possible price at the opening, which decreases in particular units in the course of the auction. The auction ends when one bidder claims willingness to pay at the standing price. The practice in Holland is done via individual-bidder buttons which are electronically connected to a big clock moving counterclockwise, indicating a decrease in price at each move of the clock hand. The bidder may at any time stop the descent of price by pushing the button and therefore stopping the clock. The first bidder to do so wins, and pays a price equivalent to the standing price at the point of the clock. Because the whole auction is quiet in the sense that no bids are tendered in the course of the auction until only at the end, one might say that there is no information passed on to the bidders present in the auction. In fact, some information are passed on to the bidders, particularly on the unwillingness to pay for the good offered at the standing price. Unlike in the English auction, there is obviously some risk involved in waiting too long for the descent of the price, because another might claim the good earlier. However, one can only claim the good at a price that is at most equal to his willingness to pay. To maximize the rent from the purchase of the good, one needs to let the price decrease low enough, but of course, at the risk that somebody else may stop the clock before. In this case, the opportunity to have any gain is lost. The information available in the English auction is thus far better in the sense that the bidder risks less (or nothing) in waiting for the standing bid to rise till it reaches his willingness to pay, after which he drops out of the game.

The other two auctions belong to the class of what is known as *sealed-bid auctions*. In the *first-price sealed bid* auction, confidential tenders are submitted simultaneously by interested parties. Whosoever has the highest bid wins and pays a price equal to his own bid. Unlike in the English and Dutch auctions, there is no information passed on to the bidders in the course of the auction. Thus, bids have to be carefully prepared, and strategic actions and conjectures about the valuations and bids of the others become a very important part of the game process. The bid submitted must balance between having a high probability of winning, which requires a higher bid, against capturing more rent, which of course requires a lower bid. In the *second-price sealed bid*, the winning bidder pays a price equivalent to the second highest bid. The strategic aspect of the game changes because of the change in the payment rule. The rent becomes the difference between what the highest bid of the opponent is and the bidder's willingness to pay. What bid to submit matters only in as far as increasing the probability of winning is concerned. The rent, which is the aspect of interest to the bidder, is unknown to the bidder until after the results have been announced.

In the following section, the theoretical modeling of the auctions is presented. The aim is to understand the strategic component of the auction game from the point of view of the bidders and the sellers. The basic framework of the benchmark model was first analyzed by Vickrey (1961).

5.1 The static Bayesian game and the Bayesian-Nash equilibrium concept [103].

A static n-player Bayesian game in the normal form is denoted by

$$GG = \{A_1,......A_n; Z_1,......Z_n; p_1,....p_n; u_1,....u_n\}$$

which specifies the players' action spaces $A_1,....A_n$, their type spaces $Z_1,....Z_n$, their beliefs $p_1,.....p_n$, and their payoff functions $u_1,......u_n$. Player i's type z_i, privately known by player i only, determines player i's payoff function, u_i $(a_1,.....a_n, z_i)$, and is a member of the set of possible types, Z_i. Player i's belief p_i $(z_{-i} \mid z_i)$ describes i's uncertainty about the n-1 other players' possible types, z_{-i}, given i's own types, z_i.

In this game, the type space Z_i is drawn by nature, and the incompleteness of information is captured by the private information held by each player on his own type z_i.

In game theory formulation, it is assumed that the game is sequenced as follows:

1) Nature draws $z = (z_1,.....z_n)$, $z_i \in Z_i$, the set of all possible types

2) Nature reveals z_i to i but not to j, $i \neq j$

3) Players simultaneously choose actions a_i from A_i

4) Payoffs are revealed $u_i(a_1,.....a_n; z_i)$

In addition to the knowledge on their own types z_i, all the players are assumed to have common knowledge of the probability distribution $p(z)$ of all the possible types $z_i = (z_1,......z_n)$.

Note that after step 2, i.e., when choosing the action a_i, the players do not have the complete history of the game. This typifies the game as one with *incomplete information*, as each of the players i do not know how much the payoffs of the other players will be, given the set of possible actions a_i $(a_1,....a_n)$, since the types z_{-i} of the

---

[103] see Gibbons (1992) p. 145 ff.

others are not known with certainty. Given that the payoff is a function of action and type, a player i formulates instead an action a_i based on his beliefs $p_i(z_{-i} \mid z_i)$ about the others' types, which is in turn based on the prior probability $p(z)$. In the continuous case, and given the independence of z_i, this belief is computed as

$$(1) \quad p_i(z_{-i}|z_i) = \frac{p(z_{-i}, z_i)}{p(z_i)} = \frac{p(z_{-i}, z_i)}{\displaystyle\int_{z_{-i} \in Z_{-i}} p(z_{-i}, z_i)}$$

where $p(z_{-i}, z_i)$ is the joint probability density function of z_i and z_{-i}, and $p(z_i)$ is nothing but the sum of the former joint densities across all other types, that is, excluding i.[104] The common knowledge assumption could thus be extended to say that each of the players i knows what the others' beliefs are about his own type z_i.

In the static Bayesian game described above, the strategies $s^* = (s_1(z_1)^*, \ldots s_n(z_n)^*)$ are a pure strategy Bayesian Nash equilibrium if for each i and for each $z_i \in Z_i, s_i^*(z_i)$ solves

$$(2) \quad \max_{a_i \in A_i} \int u_i(s_1^*(z_1), \ldots s_{i-1}^*(z_{i-1}), a_i, s_{i+1}^*(z_{i+1}), \ldots s_n^*(z_n); z) p_i(z_{-i}|z_i)$$

The equation shows that the expected utility of the player is conditional on the beliefs that he has about the others' types z_{-i}. Thus the player's objective is to find an action a_i that maximizes his utility given the optimal strategies of the others, which are in turn based on their types. Since the type of the others is not known to i, he calculates the solution based on his beliefs of the probability of the others' types.

5.2 The single unit auction game: the benchmark model

The static auction game is represented as

$$A = \{b_1, \ldots \ldots b_n; \; v_1, \ldots \ldots v_n; f_1, \ldots f_n; \; u_1, \ldots u_n\}$$

---

[104] This follows the Bayes' formula:

$$p(z_{-i}|z_i) = \frac{p(z_{-i} \cap z_i)}{p(z_i)} = \frac{p(z_{-i} \cap z_i)}{p(z_1 \cap z_i) + p(z_2 \cap z_i) + \cdots + p(z_n \cap z_i)} \quad \text{for } i = 1, \ldots n.$$

There are n participants in the game which we refer to as *bidders*, indexed as $i = 1,...n$. The types z_i in the original Bayesian game are represented by the bidders' own valuation v_i of the single object to be auctioned. This v_i is privately known to the bidders. The others do not know this information exactly, but have beliefs about this through the distribution of v_i, $\in [\underline{v}, \bar{v}]$ which is common knowledge, where $\underline{v}$ is the lowest valuation and $\bar{v}$ the highest. We shall refer to the beliefs via the density function of the valuation $f(v)$, which has a corresponding distribution function of $F(v)$, in the range $v \in [0, 1]$. Everybody else is known to have a valuation in this range. In this model, the bidders are assumed to be symmetric, each following their equilibrium bidding strategies $b_i = b_i(v_i)$.

The action a_i [105] in this model is represented by the bid offers, b_i. Here we assume that b_i is an increasing function of the valuation v_i : $b_i = b_i (v_i)$ and $b_i' (v_i) > 0$. This strategy is assumed to be common knowledge, and is fundamental to the symmetric bidding model.

5.2.1 The first-price sealed bid auction.

The bidders' pay-off is summarized by the function $u_i = u_i (v_i , b_i)$, a function of the true valuation and the bid offer b_i,. The latter represents the amount paid for winning the item. But since the bid is also a function of the v_i, we can say that ultimately, the payoff is only a function of the v_i.

The additional assumptions are as follows.

a) the v_is are independent, and hence, any additional knowledge on the others' valuation v_j , $j{\neq}i$ does not affect any bidder's valuation v_i. This shall henceforth be referred to as the auction model with independent (private) valuation.

b) the bidders are risk neutral, and have payoff functions $u_i (v_i)$, following the von Neumann-Morgenstern utility function. Its value is affected only by the true valuation v_i.

c) the seller has no reservation value, $v_0 = 0$. In addition, the seller has no additional information other than the distribution $F(v)$.

---

[105] called „message" in mechanism design theory. See chapter on mechanism design.

d) $F(v)$ is a continuous, uniform distribution in the relevant range $[0, 1]$. Thus:

(3) $\qquad F(v_i) = \dfrac{v_i - \underline{v}}{\overline{v} - \underline{v}} = v_i$

where as before, $\underline{v}$ is the lower bound and $\overline{v}$ the upper bound. The bidder's pay-off can be represented as the function[106]

(4) $\qquad u_i = u_i(v_i - b_i) = v_i - b_i \qquad\qquad \forall\, i = 1, \ldots\ldots.n$

In the game sequence discussed in the previous section, steps (1) and (2) are easy to follow using the above information. Step (3) in the auction game is represented by the simultaneous submission of the sealed bids to the seller. The seller opens these sealed envelopes and ranks the bids. The winning bidder is the one with the highest bid, and he pays a price equal to his bid. His (non-negative) payoff is immediately revealed, and the others get a zero payoff. There is no punishment for joining the game.[107]

The Nash equilibrium strategies $b_i^*(v_i)$ could be derived by solving the bidder i's objective, which is to maximize his expected utility

(5) $\qquad U_i(b_i | v_i) = u_i(v_i - b_i) \cdot \text{Prob (winning)}$

where U_i is the expected utility of a bid b_i given his valuation v_i.[108] A bid b_i^* which solves this problem is by definition in the previous section, the Bayesian-Nash equilibrium bid.

Note that this value is conditional on winning, i.e., the bidder has to calculate an action b_i that affects the U_i in two ways:

a) through the utility function u_i. A high bid lowers the value $v_i - b_i$. Thus, the lower the bid, the higher utility u_i.

b) through the probability of winning. A higher bid raises the probability of winning.

---

[106] Note that $u(v_i - b_i)$ is normalized such that $u(0) = 0$ for all i, i.e., if i does not bid, this is equivalent to submitting $b_i = 0$ such that $u_i = 0$, since $v_i = 0$.

[107] Individual Rationality assumption in mechanism design.

As is obvious in the above statements, the bidder must choose a b_i that strikes a balance between the negative effects in the payoff and the positive effects on the probability of winning.[109]

Optimal bid with $n = 2$. Let the number of bidders be $n = 2$. The probability of winning could be represented as the probability that the bid of i is higher than j, $b_i > b_j$. Assuming a linear bidding strategy of

(6) $b_i = \alpha + \beta v_i$ $\forall\, i \neq j$

Given the assumption that $b_i = 0$ when $v_i = 0$, then $\alpha = 0$ in equation (6). In addition, it is assumed that $0 < \beta \leq 1$. The highest possible bid is equal to the true valuation, such that $0 < b_i \leq 1$.

The probability of winning is thus

(7) $\mathrm{Prob}\left(b_i > b_j\right) = \mathrm{Prob}\left(\dfrac{b_i}{\beta_j} \geq v_j\right) = \dfrac{b_i}{b_j}$

And the expected payoff is

(8) $U_i\left(b_i \mid v_i\right) = u_i\left(v_i - b_i\right) \cdot \left(\dfrac{b_i}{\beta_j}\right)$

which gives an equilibrium bid of $\frac{1}{2}\, v_i$. To calculate the probability of winning, it is helpful to look at what information each bidder has. These are the distribution of v_i's, and the bidding strategy. If the bidders are symmetric, then the bidding strategy of i is the same as the bidding strategy of j. Since the bidding function is continuous in v, the probability of winning can be calculated as an inverse of the bidding function. Specifically, the probability of winning (that $b_i > b_j$) is the same as the probability of drawing a v_j that corresponds to a certain b_j such that $b_i > b_j$. But this is the same as saying that the probability of winning is the probability of drawing a v_j such that $v_i > v_j$, and this is equal to $v_i\,(b_i)$, the inverse of the bidding strategy.

---

[108] Note, however, that the bidders in the benchmark model are assumed to be risk neutral. Thus, one can use this interchangeably with the expected value maximization.

[109] Without regard as yet to risk aspects. Section 5.2 discusses the model with risk aversion.

Thus the problem of the bidder can be reformulated as:

(9) $Max_{b_i} (v_i - b_i) \cdot v_i(b_i)$

The first-order condition (FOC) is

(10) $(v_i(b_i) - b_i) \cdot v_i'(b_i) - v_i(b_i) = 0$

converting to a differential equation:

(11) $(v(b) - b) \cdot \dfrac{dv}{db} = v(b)$

(12) $(v(b) - b)dv - vdv = c$

which is an exact differential equation. Integrating:[110]

(13) $\int_0^{v_i} (v - b)dv - \int_0^{v_i} vdb = \dfrac{1}{2}(v_i - b_i)^2 + vb - \dfrac{1}{2}b_i^2 = c$

The Nash equilibrium bidding strategy is thus[111]:

(14) $b_i = \dfrac{1}{2}v_i$.

As a generalization, given n bidders, the probability of a bidder i winning the auction is the probability that all the other n-1 competitors of i draw values v_j that are less than or equal to his valuation v_i. This is represented as

(15)   Prob $(v_i \geq v_j) = v_i(b_i)^{n-1} = F(b_i)^{n-1}$ for all $i \neq j$

The general case: n bidders. The following section presents this more general case. The expected payoff of a bidder i is defined as

---

[110] again we use the justification that when $v = 0$, $b = 0$ which makes the constant of integration $c = 0$.

[111] from here we can see that $c = 0$, since $b_i = 0$ when $v_i = 0$.

(16) $U_i(b_i|v_i) = u_i(v_i - b_i) \cdot F(b_i)$

where $F(b_i)$ as discussed before, is the probability that the bid b_i is greater than the bid b_j of the competitor, $i \neq j$.

The FOC must satisfy:

(17) $U_i'(b_i^*|v_i) = F'(b_i^*) \cdot u(v_i - b_i^*) - F(b_i^*)u'(v_i - b_i^*) = 0$

where the b_i^* is the Nash equilibrium bid.

The second-order conditions must satisfy:

(18) $U_i''(b_i^*|v_i) = F''(b_i^*) \cdot u(v_i - b_i^*) - F'(b_i^*) \cdot u'(v_i - b_i^*)$

$$- F'(b_i^*) \cdot u'(v_i - b_i^*) - F(b_i^*) \cdot u''(v_i - b_i^*) < 0$$

which says that the expected payoff is at least quasi-concave in the equilibrium bid b_i^*.

Invoking the Implicit-function Theorem, equation (17) and (18) implies that there exists a differentiable function s_i such that the optimal bid b_i^* satisfies

(19) $b_i^* = s_i(v_i)$

where s_i is denoted as the strategy function or the equilibrium bid function of bidder i.

Following the FOC, we can derive the strategy function as follows:

(20) $s_i(v_i) = v_i - u_i^{-1} \left(\dfrac{u_i'(v_i - b_i^*)F(b_i^*)}{F'(b_i^*)} \right)$

where u^{-1} is the inverse of u and b_i^* is the expected EU-maximizing bid given a valuation v_i.

As discussed, because the bidders are symmetric, the probability of winning depends on the conjectures of bidder i of what the opponents j will bid based on their v_j. The optimal bid b_i of i is that which satisfies the FOC following equation (19) at a Nash equilibrium. Let $\pi(b_i^*)$ be the v-inverse of s_i, and we denote it simply by π_i.

Given n-1 rivals, the probability of winning can be written as follows:

(21) $\quad F(s_i^{-1})^{n-1} = F(\pi_i)^{n-1} = H(b_i^*)$

where s_i^{-1} is the inverse of s_i.

The EU function in (16) can be re-written as

(22) $\quad U_i = H(b_i^*)\, u_i\, (\pi_i - b_i)$

If we take the derivative of (22) with respect to π_i, and assuming linearity of the utility function,

(23) $\quad \dfrac{\partial U_i}{\partial \pi_i} = H(b_i^*) = F(\pi_i)^{n-1}$

The choice of b_i^* must satisfy (23).[112] The FOC can again be redefined as

(24) $\quad \dfrac{\partial U_i}{\partial \pi_i} \cdot \dfrac{\partial \pi_i}{\partial b_i^*} = H(b_i^*)\cdot u'(\pi_i - b_i^*)\, \pi_i' = 0$

which is just the envelope theorem. This means that any change in the expected payoff $U(\cdot)$ will be a result of a change in the bid b, but this in turn is just entirely due to the change in the (constant) valuation v.

Integrating (24) and from (22) and (23),

(25) $\quad H(b_i^*)\cdot u_i(\pi(b_i^*) - b_i^*) = \int_{x=0}^{b_i^*} H(x) u_i'(\pi(x) - x)\pi'(x)dx + c$

If $b_i = 0$, then $c = 0$ in the above equation.

Recall that the probability of winning is

(25a) $\quad F(\pi_i) = \dfrac{\pi_i}{v} = \pi_i \quad$ since $v \in [0,1]$ and $\bar{v} = 1$ is the maximum valuation.

---

[112] which is also just the expected surplus of bidder i.

Thus

(25b) $F(\pi_i)^{n-1} = H(b_i^*) = \pi_i^{n-1}$

and (24) becomes[113]

(26) $\pi_i^{n-1} \cdot (\pi_i - b_i^*) = \int_{x=0}^{b_i^*} \pi_i^{n-1}(x)\pi_i'(x)dx = \frac{1}{n}[\pi_i]^n$

The FOC is

(27) $(n-1)\pi_i^{n-2}(\pi_i - b_i^*) - \pi_i^{n-1} = 0$

and

(28) $\pi_i = b_i^* \left[\dfrac{n}{(n-1)} \right]$

or, the optimal bid is:

(29) $b_i^* = \dfrac{n-1}{n}\pi_i$

Thus, the Nash-equilibrium bid in the first-price sealed bid auction is an increasing function of the true valuation π_i. In addition, the bid increases with the number of participants n. In the two-bidder case where $n = 2$, the bid is equal to a half of the true valuation. As n approaches infinity, the bid approaches the true valuation π_i, or equivalently, v_i. This is consistent with the theory of competition, that is, the more participants there are in the bidding game, the closer is the equilibrium price to the true willingness to pay. As a consequence, the rent extracted becomes small, until it vanishes in the case of infinite number of participants.

---

[113] Since $\dfrac{\partial u}{\partial \pi} = 1$

To illustrate further, suppose i believes that all other bidders will bid according to the function in (29). The maximum bid in our model would then be $\bar{b} = \dfrac{n-1}{n} \cdot \bar{v}_i$. The v-inverse of b will be

(30) $\pi_i = \left(\dfrac{n}{n-1}\right) \cdot b_i$

Thus the probability that all other bidders will bid less than or equal to $b*$ is

(31) $F(\pi_i)^{n-1} = H(b*) = \left[\left(\dfrac{n}{n-1}\right) b_i\right]^{n-1}$

The expected utility of bidder i is thus:

(32) $U_i(b_i* \mid \pi_i) = H(b_i*) \cdot u(\pi_i - b_i*) = \left[\left(\dfrac{n}{n-1}\right) b_i\right]^{n-1} \cdot (\pi_i - b_i*)$

the FOC is

(33) $(n-1)\left(\dfrac{n}{n-1}\right)^{n-1} b_i^{n-2}(\pi_i - b_i) - \left(\dfrac{n}{n-1}\right)^{n-1} b_i^{n-1} = 0$

and the equilibrium bid is

(34) $b_i^* = \left(\dfrac{n-1}{n}\right)\pi_i$

With the generalization of a distribution of valuation in the range $[\underline{v}, \bar{v}]$, the Nash-equilibrium bid function is represented by

(35) $b_i = \underline{v} + \dfrac{n-1}{n}(v_i - \underline{v})$ for all $i = 1, \dots \dots n$

and the highest bid is thus

$$(36) \quad \bar{b} = \underline{v} + \frac{n-1}{n}(\bar{v} - \underline{v})$$

The implication of this result is that in the case of a finite n, the highest bid in the first-price sealed bid auction is less than the highest valuation. In fact, all Nash-equilibrium bids are less than the bidders' true valuation. The first-price sealed bid is therefore *not* a truth-revealing auction; it involves a formation of a bidding strategy where the bidders shade their bids to be able to capture some rent. However, the more participants there are in the bidding game, the greater is the probability that any other bidder $j \neq i$ will have a bid that is higher than that of i. Thus, the bidder must increase his bid to compensate for the increased risk of losing the game and coming out empty. The winner is the bidder with the highest valuation, but his payment, which is also his bid, will be less than this.

5.2.2 The second price sealed bid auction.

As was already discussed before, the second price sealed bid differs from the first price sealed bid in the amount of payment upon winning. Specifically, the winning bidder pays a price that is equal to the second highest bid (or, which amounts to the same thing, the highest rejected bid). Let $x \in [\underline{x}, \bar{x}]$ be the variable representing the highest bids of all the other bidders $j = 1,....n$ with cumulative distribution $G_i(x)$. The bidder's expected payoff in a two-bidder game can be represented as

$$(37) \quad U_i(b_i \,|\, v_i) = \int_{x=\underline{x}}^{b_i} (v_i - x) \cdot dG_i(x)$$

The equilibrium bid $b_i{}^*$ must satisfy the first-order conditions:

$$(38) \quad U_i'(b_i^* \,|\, v_i) = (v_i - b_i^*) \cdot G_i'(b_i^*) = 0$$

which means that the Nash-equilibrium bid is[114]

$$(39) \quad b_i^* = v_i$$

---

[114] since $G'(b_i) \neq 0$.

95

This shows that the second price sealed bid auction is a truth-revealing auction, as the bids are equal to the actual valuation of the bidders. In other words, the dominant strategy of the bidder is to bid his true (maximum) valuation, as the probability of winning depends on his own bid, but the payment is not. By doing so, he increases his chance of winning, but due to the symmetry assumption, the expected payment is less than the equilibrium bid. The winner will be the one with the highest valuation, and the price to be paid is the second highest valuation, thus still allowing him to capture some rent.

5.2.3 The Dutch auction

The Dutch auction is a decreasing bid procedure, wherein the bids decrease as the auction progresses, or as the clock ticks. It can thus be formulated that the standing bid b_i is a function of the elapsed time t, such that

(40) $\quad b(t_1) > b(t_2)$ for all t_k, $k = 1,...K$ where $t_1 < t_2 < t_3 < ..... < t_K$

The problem of the bidder is to assess when at best to stop the clock, or, in what amounts to the same thing, when to accept the standing bid.

Let $F_i(b(t))$ be bidder i's subjective probability assessment, at the beginning of the auction, that he will win by accepting the standing bid $b(t)$. His expected payoff is

(41) $\quad U(b(t)) = u(v_i - b(t)) \cdot F(b(t))$

The bidder has a plan, at the beginning of the auction, to accept a bid $b_i(t_k^*)$ that maximizes (41). The optimal time for a bidder i to stop the clock is when

(42) $\quad \left(\left[u(v_i - \frac{b(t_k^*)) \cdot F_i'(b(t_k^*))}{F_i(b(t_k^*))} \right] - u'(v_i - b(t_k^*)) \right) \cdot b'(t_k^*) = 0$

where $t_k^* \in (0, K)$, k ranges from the beginning (0) to the maximum time K allowed in the auction. The equation may also be simplified by just equating the terms in the large brackets to zero, as the term outside the bracket, the change in the standing bid, is negative. As one might notice, this is very similar to the FOC in the first price auction

The equilibrium bid, as in the first price auction, is therefore not truth revealing. The bidder will plan to stop the clock at a point below his true willingness to pay, v_i. If the bidding strategies are again symmetric, then any bidder i will employ the same strategy in the first price auction as in the Dutch auction. In this case, the two auctions are said to be *isomorphic*, i.e., having the same strategic element.

5.2.4 The English auction

The English auction can be analyzed in a much easier way. Remember that this auction ensures a constant flow of information on the standing bids, which are increasing. As long as the standing bid is below his valuation, he stays in the game. Since there is a constant flow of information, the bidder can afford to set a dominant strategy such that he drops out at the latest when the next bid already exceeds his valuation.[115] In this case, the valuations are revealed truthfully; there is no incentive to keep on raising the bid if this anyway already exceeds the true valuation. The equilibrium price will be equal to at least the second highest valuation, and at most plus the bid margin ε. Thus, in terms of the strategic element of the game, it is said to be isomorphic with the second price sealed bid auction.

On the basis of the previous results on isomorphism, the following analysis will be limited to the sealed bid auction, particularly first-price sealed bid, unless otherwise indicated. This allows a thorough understanding of the strategic element of the bidding process in the existence of variations in the assumptions in benchmark model.[116]

5.3 Effects of risk aversion.

Let the utility function of a bidder i be represented as

$$(43) \quad U_i(b_i \mid v_i, r_i) = u(v_i - b_i) \cdot F(b_i) = (v_i - b_i)^{r_i} \cdot F(b_i)$$

---

[115] or the earliest when the standing bid is equal to his valuation.

[116] In some sections, references to open-auctions might be made. Note that since the outcome of the second price sealed bid and English auctions represent dominant strategy equilibrium, it is expected that the results will be invariant to the index of risk aversion. This is the reason why the analysis in the next section is limited to the first price sealed bid auction.

where $r_i \in [0,1]$, with $1 - r_i$ as the Arrow-Pratt measure of constant relative risk aversion.[117]

Note that each bidder i has private information about his own r_i, but knows only that the others' r_j is drawn from the probability distribution Θ with support $[0,1]$. This is the general Ledyard-type model where the *pdf* Θ is not assumed to have a density function, meaning that each bidder i can have a mass of probability 0 or 1. The model includes all types of risk aversion, i.e., risk neutral and risk averse.

The FOC must again satisfy equation (17). However, note that the bidding function is not just a function of v_i, but also of r_i:

$$(44) \quad b_i^* = s_i(v_i, r_i)$$

Thus, the strategy function in (20) could be defined as

$$(45) \quad s_i(v_i, r_i) = \frac{n-1+r_i}{n-1} b_i - \frac{r_i}{n-1} \underline{v}$$

As in (8), let $\pi(b_i^*, r_i)$ be the v-inverse of s_i. The probability of winning is the probability that any value b is greater than b_i, i.e., the probability that bidder i draws a value v_i and r_i that represents a bid b_i less than b. As in the analysis with risk-neutral bidders in the first-price auction, the value of the highest bid must be less than the value of the highest valuation $\bar{v}$.

Using the notation employed earlier, for the two player case,

$$(46) \quad F(b) = E_r\left[\frac{\pi(b,r)}{\bar{v} - \underline{v}}\right] = \int_0^1 \int_{\underline{v}}^{\pi}(b_i, r_i) \frac{dv \, d\Theta(r_i)}{(\bar{v} - \underline{v})} = \left[\frac{n-1+E(r)}{(n-1)(\bar{v} - \underline{v})}\right](b_i - \underline{v})$$

For the n-player case, this probability is

---

[117] The Arrow-Pratt absolute risk aversion measure can be summarized as $-\dfrac{U''(W)}{U'(W)}$ where W is wealth.

Although the ratio is decreasing in W, when multiplied by W, the measure becomes constant through the values of W, thus the name constant relative risk aversion.

$$(47) \quad F(b)^{n-1} = \left[\frac{n-1+E(r)}{(n-1)(\bar{v}-\underline{v})} \right]^{n-1} (b_i - \underline{v})^{n-1}$$

Since $\underline{v} = 0$, then

$$(48) \quad H(b_i) = \left[\underset{r}{E}(\pi(b_i, r_i)) \right]^{n-1} \cdot \left[\pi(b_i, r_i) - b_i \right]^{r_i}$$

$$= \int_0^{b_i} \left[\underset{r}{E}(\pi(x, r)) \right]^{n-1} r_i \left[\pi_i(x, r_i) - x \right]^{r_i - 1} \pi(x, r_i) dx$$

And the equilibrium bids are

$$(49) \quad b(v_i, r_i) = \frac{n-1}{n-1+r_i} v_i$$

Or more generally,

$$(50) \quad b(v_i, r_i) = \underline{v} + \frac{n-1}{n-1+r_i} (v_i - \underline{v})$$

The highest bid is therefore equal to

$$(51) \quad \bar{b}(\bar{v}, r_i) = \underline{v} + \frac{n-1}{n-1+r_i} (\bar{v} - \underline{v})$$

Given the assumed distribution of r_i, a risk averse bidder (where $0 < r_i < 1$) will always bid higher than a risk-neutral bidder. Note that these bid functions have generally shifted upwards with bidders that are risk averse. Thus, the average bids have increased.

The explanation for this is that risk averse individuals need to insure themselves against the risk of losing. But the only way to do this is to increase the bids, which increases the probability of winning. This is of course commensurate to a decrease in the pay-off, as the higher the bid, the higher will be the payment. The difference between the equilibrium bids in the benchmark model and this model is the risk premium – what the bidder pays in addition to cover the risk of coming out empty.

5.4 Sales Revenue

In the preceding section, we have discussed some elements of the revenue aspects of the auction game. In this section, an analysis of the seller behavior is done. In most cases, it is quite realistic to assume that sellers are out to make revenue, such that the higher the revenue provided by a certain type of auctions, the more appealing it is to the auctioneer. It might be more correct to say that this is true for most private auction, or auctions involving the buying or selling of private goods, i.e., wherever exclusion in consumption applies.

On the basis of the results in the previous section, the probability distribution of the sales price p in the first price sealed bid benchmark auction could be represented as:

$$(52) \quad F(p) = \left[\frac{n-1+E(r)}{(n-1)(\bar{v}-\underline{v})} \right]^n (p-\underline{v})^n$$

within the relevant range. The highest bid is as indicated in equation (51), $\bar{b}$, and the lowest bid is equal to $\underline{v}$. The expected price is thus

$$(53) \quad \bar{p} = \int_{\underline{v}}^{\bar{b}} p \, dF(p) = \left[\frac{n-1+E(r)}{n} \right]^n \cdot \left[\frac{(n-1)(\bar{v}-\underline{v})}{n+1} + \underline{v} \right]$$

From the formula, it is clear that the expected revenue increases with increasing risk aversion. In the limiting case when n approaches infinity and $E(r) = 0$, the expected selling price is equivalent to the selling price in the benchmark model, which is in turn, equal to the selling price in the second-price sealed bid auction.[118]

---

[118] Based on the order statistics, i.e., that the expected selling price is the expected value of the second highest bid.

5.4.1 No reservation fees.

In the benchmark auction model where the bidders are risk neutral, the four auction institutions yield the same revenue on the average.[119]

Vickrey (1961) is the first to establish this. To show this, we refer to the case where we have $v \in [0,1]$ and risk neutral bidders such that $E(r) = 1$. The expected revenue is reduced to the form:

$$(54) \quad \bar{p} = pdF(p) = \left[\frac{n}{n}\right]^n \cdot \left[\frac{(n-1)(\bar{v})}{n+1}\right]$$

Given the assumptions of the benchmark model, this is equivalent to 1/3 in a two-bidder model.

5.4.2 With reservation fees.

The introduction of reservation fees have the initial effect of adjusting the distribution function of valuation. To illustrate, imagine an auction of say, a famous painting. It has already been pre-announced that the minimum acceptable bid for the painting will be $2.0 million, but of course without an upper limit. What might be expected to happen? Surely if I would have an excess of $1.0 million for which I planned to spend on buying the painting, I will be automatically dropped out of the auction even before it started. Thus, only those who are willing to pay at least 2.0 million will go to the auction. But it may very well be that nobody is willing to pay such money for the painting. If nobody attends the auction, then the reservation price is much too high, and there is a breakdown of the auction. If there is a second date for the auction, the reservation price will have to be lowered.

Several conclusions are immediate in this small illustration. First, that by setting a reserve price, the auctioneer discriminates against the low-valuation bidders such that they do not have to attend the auction and waste the precious auction time by starting with a too low bid. Second, the expected selling price increases.

---

[119] The additional assumption is that the reservation price of the seller is zero.

Suppose that the reservation price of the seller is increased from 0 to 0.5 in the benchmark model. The optimal bid is expected to shift up, with the y-intercept starting at the lowest acceptable valuation $\underline{v} = 0.5$. The bidding function becomes steeper than before, and this means that the bid given the same valuation as before would be relatively higher. The Nash equilibrium bids can be represented as:

$$(55) \quad b(v_i, r_i) = 0.5 + \frac{n-1}{n-1+r_i}(v_i - 0.5)$$

From equation (52), this can be shown by changing the $\underline{v}$ from zero to 0.5:

$$(56) \quad F(p) = \left[\frac{n-1+E(r)}{(n-1)(\bar{v}-0.5)}\right]^n (p-0.5)^n$$

and from (53)

$$(57) \quad \bar{p} = \int_{\underline{v}}^{\bar{b}} p\,dF(p) = \left[\frac{n-1+E(r)}{n}\right]^n \cdot \left[\frac{(n-1)(\bar{v}-0.5)}{n+1} + 0.5\right].$$

Under risk neutrality, and from (54)

$$(58) \quad \bar{p} = \int_{0.5}^{\bar{b}} p\,dF(p) = \left[\frac{n}{n}\right]^n \cdot \left[\frac{(n-1)(\bar{v}-0.5)}{n+1} + 0.5\right] = \frac{n-1}{n+1}(0.5) + 0.5 = 2/3$$

which is higher than the original expected revenue of 1/3.

The problem, however, is that there is now a positive probability that the seller ends up with the item, i.e., that it is not sold. This is inefficient, especially if the seller has a true reservation price of zero. By increasing the reservation price, the expected revenue increases, but at the risk of not having sold the item.

5.5 Affiliated Valuation and the Winner's Curse

The analysis in the benchmark model has assumed that the valuations are *private information* and known with certainty by the individual bidders. This is one extreme case. The other extreme case is that the value of the good being auctioned *is not known with certainty*. Since they do not have the information on the true value of the object, the bidders must formulate an *estimate* of this value in order to submit a rational bid.

There are two possible cases in which this situation could be modeled. One is the case where there is a re-sale market for the good, and the resale price is not known with certainty because one knows only the possible range of prices that the good can fetch in the market. The other case is when the uncertainty in valuation comes from incomplete information about the variables that affect the true valuation of the good being sold. These informational variables may be say, the characteristics of the good which determine how much its value will be in the market.

In the analysis of these types of goods, it is assumed that the object has an objective true value, V, which is the same for all of the bidders. Since this V is unknown to all, each bidder i must form an estimate of the value of the object. To do this, the bidder will have to take some samples from a population of information or *signals* of the possible value of the object. These signals are drawn from a commonly known distribution. Although the true objective value of the good is the same across the bidders, their estimates could vary, and the variation depends on the degree of the differences in the quality and quantity of information that each of the bidders have collected. This section will discuss the analytics of such types of goods, which the literature calls the *common values model*. The phenomenon of the winner's curse will be firstly discussed as an introduction to show the major differences between the independent private values model and the common values model. The discussion will then proceed to a more general formulation of the model, using the affiliated valuation.

5.5.1 The winner's curse

Many experimental studies[120] have been conducted on the topic of the common value auction. The main driving force for these investigations is the great interest in explaining the phenomenon called *"the winner's curse"*, which is observed in many common value auctions. The following is quoted from Thaler (1992, p.50), and gives an amusing picture of the phenomenon:

> *Next time you find yourself a little short of cash for a night on the town, try the following experiment in your neighborhood tavern. Take a jar and fill it with coins, noting the total value of the coins. Now auction off the jar to the assembled masses at the bar (offering to pay the winning bidder in bills to control for penny aversion). Chances are very high that the following results will be obtained:*
>
> *1. The average bid will be significantly less than the value of the coins (bidders are risk averse)*
>
> *2. The winning bid will* **exceed** *the value of the [coins in the] jar.*
>
> *In conducting this demonstration, you will have simultaneously obtained the funding necessary for your evening's entertainment and enlightened the patrons about the perils of the "winner's curse".*

The basic framework of the game leading to the problem of winners curse is the fact that the bidders did not know exactly what the value of the coins in the jar is. To make a reasonable estimate, they probably have examined the contents of the jar. Given that there are enough coins in the jar to prevent one from making an exact count, the offers or bids for the jar will generally be distributed over a reasonable range of values. The value estimate that each of the potential bidders has will be conditioned on the individual's *signal*, or his judgement based on the observed contents of the jar.

In general, each bidder is expected to submit a bid that is formed by "discounting" the value estimate by a certain factor, $0 \le \delta \le 1$ in order to allow them to capture some profit, in the event that they win. A bid is submitted that will give him the highest expected payoff.[121] Despite this, *upon confirming that he won*, the winning bidder

---

[120] See Samuelson and Bazerman (1985), Lind and Plott (1991), Hansen and Lott (1991), Garvin and Kagel (1994) among others, for reports on auction experiments with common values.

[121] Assuming rationality. This is the aim of each of the bidders.

finds surprisingly that he *overbids*, and suffers from a negative payoff, a *curse* that he has to live with. But this is something that he did not expect *before* tendering the bid.

The winner's curse is in general to be expected in auctions in which the true value of the good is unknown. A classic example is the auction of mineral rights. [122] Before *i* submits a bid, he ought to collect some data on the potential value of the oil that could be extracted. It is either that the bidder himself makes an estimate of the value, or an independent expert is engaged to conduct a reliable estimate.

As in the previous auction, Thaler (1992) says that the winner in a common value auction is cursed in two ways:

a) the value of the mineral resource is much less than the bid for the rights, resulting in negative profits; and

b) the expert estimates are usually *higher* than the actual value of the resource.

To study the effect of the winner's curse, Bazerman and Samuelson (1983) conducted a series of experiment very much similar to the game presented above by Thaler (1992). Their results confirm the statements above. The value of the coins totaled $8.00, but the *average winning bid* in the series of experiment was $10.01. Kagel and Levin (1986) also proved the existence of the winner's curse in their experimental studies. Thiel (1988), on the other hand, tried to show that if the bidders are rational

---

[122] Another example of a common value auction in practice is the award of public works contracts. A contractor offers to provide a combination of labor and material inputs to a government project at minimum cost. The supplier knows exactly what the *current costs* of the labor and materials are. On the basis of the information prior to the implementation of the project, he could make an estimate of the cost of the inputs which will apply at the time of implementation. He offers a rational bid such that he gets the maximum expected returns from the contract. If he wins, he will know that he had offered the lowest price for the contract, possibly because he had underestimated the possible future cost of the inputs. When contract implementation starts, his information set - which was the basis of his bid - takes a new form. A higher rate of inflation (than what was expected) at the time of the actual purchase of materials for construction raises the cost of the contract, and lowers the profit. Other uncertain cases may include the attitude of workers, i.e., the usual principal-agent problems like shirking from work, which increases the actual labor requirements to complete the job. Unless renegotiations for additional unexpected costs are open in the contract, the winning bidder will always face a positive probability of having lower profits, or even losing, which is again a winner's curse.

and follow the Nash equilibrium bids, the winner's curse should in principle not exist.[123]

In the common value auction, the average bid is found out to be lower than the actual value of the coins. The highest bidder loses because he offers a bid higher than the *actual value* of the coins in the jar, resulting either from an overestimate of the value, or an overestimate of the bids of the competing bidders. This despite the fact that the expected value, given the signal of each bidder (i.e., including the highest bidder) is an unbiased estimate of the true value of the good.[124]

The phenomenon of winner's curse may be considered to be counter-intuitive. It is in general not individually rational to have a bidder submit a bid that makes him lose *in the event that he wins*. If he expects to lose, the bidder should not submit a bid at all (therefore he is guaranteed his original utility). Submitting a bid b means that the bidder has *a priori* calculated his expected payoff to be positive, and the chosen bid b maximizes his payoff.[125] Put differently, prior to having the information on who wins, the bidder *did not expect* to lose in the event he wins.

The reason behind is the difference in the information base *before* and *after* the bidding. Recall that the value estimates are conditional on the *prior information* derived by sampling. The bidder has to make a bid offer based on the signals of the

---

[123] In many of the experimental studies conducted so far on the behavior of bidders in a common value auction, a simple model similar to that presented in Garvin and Kagel (1994) was often used. The true value of the good V is distributed as in the interval $(\underline{V}, \overline{V})$ and this is common knowledge to the bidders. Each bidder makes an estimate of the value V by drawing a signal $s \in S$ from the commonly known distribution $(\underline{V} + \varepsilon, \overline{V} - \varepsilon)$, where ε is also commonly known. The equilibrium bids for the risk neutral bidders are: $b(s_i) = s_i - \varepsilon + Y$ where $Y = \frac{2\varepsilon}{n+1} e^{-\frac{n}{2\varepsilon}(s_i - (\underline{V} + \varepsilon))}$ and n is the number of bidders The signal s_i on the possible value of V which each of the bidders $i = 1,....n$ has, is an unbiased estimate of the value V. Thus for the bid function to be an increasing function of s_i, the first term on the right hand side should be greater than the sum of the last two terms, for all i. The bidder with the highest signal $\overline{s}_i$ in this *symmetric* model will also have the highest bid $\overline{b}_i$. This can be verified to be a consequence of the symmetry of information that enters the equation represented by Y. Given independence of S, the highest signal will more likely be an overestimate, and the rate of overestimation or *bias* increases with n. The equation, being a Nash equilibrium bid, must already consider this possible bias and must therefore reflect a downward adjustment of the bid conditional on s_i being the maximum of all the possible estimates, i.e., the highest of the order statistics of signals.

[124] see Thiel (1988) p. 884. He claims that it is important to distinguish between the bidders' estimation problems and the bidding problem. In any case, he claims that the winner's curse results from a failure to optimize correctly.

[125] If the bidders have an optimizing behavior in the sense of Nash, then a Nash equilibrium bid will predict a positive profit.

characteristics of the good sampled, which then determine its value. On the other hand, winning itself is an informative event. It conveys the information that the winner has the highest value estimate among all the bidders; the reason why the bidder won. The value estimate, although unbiased, is the *upper bound of all the estimates*, and would therefore have a positive probability of being an overestimate. Whether or not it is theoretically justifiable on the basis of Nash equilibrium strategies, this phenomenon is nevertheless observed in many common value auctions.

Milgrom (1989) claims that for the common value auction, the estimate across all the bidders of the value of the good is *positively correlated*, although the estimation errors are *independent*. This is attributable to a commonality facing the bidders in as far as the uncertainty of the factors that determine the estimates of the good is concerned. This, he claims, is the main reason for the existence of the winner's curse. Milgrom and Weber (1982) present the following to illustrate the winner's curse in a model of a common value auction. Suppose the sale of a particular good is a common value first-price auction. The winning bid thus becomes the price of the mineral rights. Since this price comes from the bid of the winning bidder, this information might be considered to be nothing new to him. However, there is new information to him because he confirms that he has the highest bid.[126]

Winkler and Brooks (1980) model a common value auction where the estimation errors are dependent.[127] Their results showed that the dependence of estimation errors decreases the probability of the winning bidder suffering from winner's curse, but this is only for bidders with small error variances. The reverse is true for bidders with large error variances. Thus, bidders with large estimation error variances which also violate Milgrom's assumption on independence of errors face a high probability of suffering from the winner's curse.

---

[126] In particular, let $f(x| V = v)$ be the density function of the estimates which is assumed to have the so-called monotone likelihood ratio property (MLRP). Given two possible estimates v_1 and v_2, where $v_1 < v_2$, the ratio $f(x| v_1) / f(x| v_2)$ is decreasing in x. In the limit, i.e., as the ratio approaches zero, the equilibrium price in this auction given many bidders is a consistent estimator of the true value V, even if no single bidder i can alone estimate V efficiently on the basis of his own private information. Following MLRP, the winning bid has an estimate which is the highest among all the estimate.

[127] Thus violating Milgrom's assumption.

5.5.2 A generalization: the affiliated values model

In reality, most goods will be a mixture of both independent private values and common values. Some goods could have more common value features and the others could have more independent private value features. For instance, it is possible to imagine a zealous bidder for a mineral oil rights whose family tradition it is to be in the oil business. Whereas the true value of the oil will in general be the same across the bidders, this particular bidder will have an additional private value component which raises his valuation a little over the unbiased estimate of the value of the oil that could be extracted. The analysis of this kind of a good was pioneered by Milgrom and Weber (1982) in a model with *affiliated valuation*, which is to be discussed in the following.

Unlike the case when the estimation errors are independent, in the general symmetric model presented by Milgrom and Weber (1982), the estimation errors can be positively correlated. There exists a vector $X = (X_1, X_2,....X_n)$ whose *components* are real-valued informational variables, either in the form of *value estimates* or *signals* on the good, and these are observed by the individual bidders. Next, there is a vector of real valued variables, $S = (S_1, S_2,...S_m)$, which affect the (common) value of the object to the bidders. Some components of these are observable to the seller, in the form of, say, independent expert estimates. The value of the object to the bidder depends both on his private signals as well as other variables which he may or may not observe at the time he wants to submit his bid.

The utility of the individual is represented as the function[128] :

(59) $U_i = u_i(s_i, x_i) \quad \forall \ i = 1,.....n$

The following are also assumed:

a) $\exists$ a function $u \in R^{m+n}$: $\forall \ i, \ u_i (S, X) = u (S, X_i, \{X_j\} \ j \neq i)$. This means that the *valuations* depend on S in the *same manner*, but there is a private information component which is captured by the variable x_i. This is the symmetry assumption.

---

[128] The utility function of the individual will be represented as $U_i = u_i (S, X)$ in the general case, and in the case of a risk neutral bidder as $V_i = v_i (S, X)$.

b) $u_i \geq 0$, $u' > 0$, $u'' < 0$. The bidder is guaranteed at least his original utility. The utility function increases in its arguments, and is well-behaved and twice differentiable.

c) $E(V_i) < \infty$ $\forall$ i. This says that the expected value is finite.

Note that if $m = 0$, the model collapses into an independent private values model where each bidder has a true valuation that is equal to his own private information, i.e., $v_i = x_i$. The information that the bidder has on the object is exactly his true (private) valuation of the object. In the common values model, the S vector reduces to a single variable, $m = 1$ and $v_i = s_i$. Thus the value of the object to the bidder is exactly that which is determined by the variable s, which maybe an expert's estimate of the value of the object, or his own estimate as shown in the previous section.

Nature assigns each bidder i a pair of variables $\{v_i, x_i\}$ denoted by

(60) $z = \{v_i, x_i\}$

which is real-valued and has a distribution function F (z), and a density function f (z)[129]. The density f (z) is a joint density function of $\{v_i, x_i\}$, representing the probability that a bidder of type z has the private information x_i and a corresponding valuation v_i. A very important theorem in this model of auction is the so-called affiliation, which is discussed below.

Theorem. (Milgrom and Weber, 1982). Given a vector $Z = (Z_1, \ldots Z_n)$ with a corresponding distribution F (z) and density function f (z), the variables $Z_1, \ldots Z_n$ are affiliated if for any $z, z' \in Z$ which are in $\mathbf{R}^{m+n}$,

(61) $f(z \wedge z') f(z \vee z') \geq f(z) f(z')$

where $z \wedge z'$ and $z \vee z'$ are the component-wise minimum and maximum of z, respectively.

---

[129] with support being a rectangular cell $\mathbf{Z} = \{z| \underline{z}\mathbf{1} \leq z \leq \overline{z}\mathbf{1}\}$, where $\mathbf{1}$ is an indicator function.

The above can be interpreted simply as a case where large values for the other variables are more likely when one variable already takes a large value.[130] In this case, the estimation errors for the value of the good are positively correlated. In independent values model, where the random variables X are statistically independent, there is a strict equality of (61), and affiliation is satisfied trivially.[131]

Milgrom and Weber (1982) formally presents the affiliation of the variables through a series of theorems, which are summarized as follows:

a) Let f: $R^n \rightarrow$ R. f is affiliated iff $\dfrac{\partial^2 \ln f}{\partial z_i \partial z_j} \geq 0 \forall i \neq j$.

b) If $f(z) = g(z)\, h(z)$ where g and h are nonnegative and affiliated (in the sense of (a) above), then f is affiliated.

c) If $Z_1,.....Z_n$ are affiliated and $g_1,.....g_n$ are all nondecreasing functions (or non-increasing functions), then $g_1(Z_1),....g_k(Z_n)$ are affiliated.

The above theorems are useful to prove that the conditional expected value of the payoff

(62) $E\ (V_1 \mid X_1 = x^1, X_2 = x^2 .... X_n = x^n\ )$

is nondecreasing in x, where x^1, x^2 .... x^n are the values of $\mathbf{X}$ arranged from highest to lowest. In a common values model, given the two highest values x^1 and x^2, a bidder i will win when[132]

(63) $V_i(\rho) = E\ (v_i \mid x_i = x^1 = \rho;\ x^2 < \rho)$

---

[130] An example of a case where the strict inequality applies in practice is in the case of a sale of painting. If an individual places a high value on say, an art by Rembrandt (maybe because he appreciates it so much), it is also likely that the others have the same deep appreciation of the painting, thereby also putting a high value on it.

[131] To understand the notion, it may be helpful to clarify the notation. Let $z = (x_i, v_i)$, and let x, $v \in \{0,1\}$. Thus we have the set $\mathbf{Z} = \{(0,0), (0,1), (1,0), (1,1)\}$ which is defined as the set in $\mathbf{R}^2$. Let z, $z' \in \mathbf{R}^2$ be points in $\mathbf{Z}$. By definition, we have $(z \wedge z') = (0,0)$ and $(z \vee z') = (1,1)$. By the affiliation theorem, we have $f(0,0)\, f(1,1) \geq f(0,1)\, f(1,0)$. This helps to establish that a bidder with a high value estimate x_i will also have a high valuation. This is further extended to include the affiliation of the signals s, value estimates x and valuation v_i, i.e., that a bidder with a high signal s_i will more likely have a high estimate x_i and thus a high valuation v_i.

[132] see Wilson (1992) p. 233.

110

Thus, given two values $x_i = \rho$ and $x_j < \rho$ bidder i bids lower than in the case when $x_i = \rho$ and $x_j = \rho$. The case when $x_i = x_j = \rho$ is the upper bound of bidder i's value (and bid), conditional on this signal that is available to him. In the following, the first price sealed bid auction will be used to illustrate the equilibrium outcome in the affiliated values model, assuming risk neutrality.

The expected utility of the bidder could then be represented as:

(64) $\quad U_i(b_i|v_i) = (v_i(x_i, s) - b_i(v_i)) \cdot \text{Prob}(winning)$

where, as before, x and s are assumed to be affiliated.

As before, the probability of winning is the probability that bidder i submits a b_i that is the highest among all the bids submitted

(65) $\quad$ Prob $(winning) = $ Prob $(b_i \geq b_j) = F_{\max}(b_i) = F_1(b_i) F_2(b_i).....F_{n-1}(b_i)$

which is equal to $F(b_i)^{n-1}$ by symmetry.[133] Note that to have a high bid, bidder i must have had the highest signal $x^1 = \rho$, while all the others have signals less   than ρ.

The conditional density of the second highest value x^2 given that $x^1 = \rho$ is denoted as $f(x^2 = \tau | x^1 = \rho)$ or simply as $f(\tau | \alpha)$. Thus the probability of winning is the probability that the others have a lower signal denoted by

(66) $\quad F(b_i)^{n-1} = F_{x2}(x^2 = \tau | x^1 = \rho) = F_{x2}(\tau | \rho)$

Given the assumption on the Nash equilibrium bidding strategies, the optimal bidding functions have an inverse which is denoted by $\pi(b^*)$. For the particular individual i, his objective is to maximize the expected pay-off

(67) $\quad [v(x, \tau) - b] F_{x2}(\tau | x)$

where $\tau < \rho$, the value of the signal of the next highest valuation x^2.

Using the notation in the previous section, the expected payoff can be written as

---

[133] Let $M = \max(X_1,.....X_n)$ where $X_1,....X_n$ are independent random variables. The distribution of M, $F_{\max}(x)$ is given by $F_1(x) F_2(x).....F_n(x)$.

(68) $U_i(b|v_i, x) = \int_{\underline{x}}^{\pi(b)} (v(x^1, \tau) - b) f_{x^2}(\tau|x^1 = \rho) d\tau$

for a risk-neutral bidder i, which is to be maximized with respect to b. The FOC is

(69) $0 = -F_{x^2}(\pi(b)|\rho) + \left[v(x^1, \pi(b)) - b\right] \cdot f_{x^2}(\pi(b)|\rho) \cdot \pi'(b)$

Note that in equilibrium, $b = \pi^{-1}(\rho)$; $\pi'(b) = \dfrac{1}{\pi^{-1}(\rho)} = \dfrac{1}{b^{*\prime}(\rho)}$ so that the FOC can be

reformulated as

(70) $0 = -F_{x^2}(\rho|\rho) + \left[v(\rho, \rho) - b^*(\rho)\right] \cdot f_{x^2}(\rho|\rho) \cdot 1/b^{*\prime}(\rho)$

(71) $b^{*\prime}(\rho) = \left[v(\rho, \rho) - b^*(\rho)\right] \dfrac{f_{x^2}(\rho|\rho)}{F_{x^2}(\rho|\rho)}$

which is a necessary condition. The second term on the right is assumed to be zero outside the range of possible values of s.

The equilibrium bidding strategy is shown by Milgrom and Weber (1982) as

(72) $b^*(x) = \int_{\underline{\rho}}^{s} v(\tau, \tau) dL(\tau|x)$

where $L(\tau| x) = \exp\left(\int_{x=\tau}^{\rho} \dfrac{f_{x^2}(x|x)}{F_{x^2}(x|x)}\right)$

Equation (72) takes the general form[134]

(72a) $b^*(x) = v(x,x) - \int_{\underline{\rho}}^{\rho} L(\tau|x) dv(\tau, \tau)$

The proof of the above can be found in Milgrom and Weber (1982).

---

[134] This may also be written in the form $b^*(x) = \min \{\rho, E\{\max [r, x^2] | x^1 = \rho\}\}$, where r is th seller's reserve price.

112

One thing that must be noted in the model with correlated valuations is the effect on efficiency. First, that in the symmetric model, the bidder with the highest (estimated) valuation wins. This is thus efficient. However, in the presence of high uncertainty in the value of the good, the winner's curse, if it exists, may lead to a situation of inefficiency. So far, the literature is scant on the solution to this problem. The approach taken is to inform the bidders of the possible existence of the problem, so that each potential bidder will be aware of it in the process of formulating a bid. The result is of course a downward adjustment of all the bids, which, in this case, corrects the bias in the auction game. Whereas before, it was shown by various experimental studies that the average winning bids in a repeated common value auction is higher than the true value of the good sold, providing the information that leads to a downward adjustment of the bids should lead to an average winning bid whose value approaches the true value of the good. The inefficiency created by ignorance that leads to too heated bidding need not exist, but the winner remains to be the one with the highest value estimate.

5.6 Multiple-unit auctions

5.6.1 Independent private values model

A year after the seminal paper of Vickrey (1961) on the benchmark auction model, he extended the analysis[135] to a case of an auction with multiple units q of the goods to be sold to n risk-neutral agents; $1 \leq q \leq n$. Like the benchmark model, the valuations of the individual bidders are assumed to be uniformly distributed over a range $[\underline{v}, \bar{v}]$. Later, Harris and Raviv (1981) have extended Vickrey's multiple-unit model to include a general form of a distribution function for the valuation, as well as concave utility functions.[136]

In the original analysis undertaken, each bidder acquires only one unit of the good. In this framework, it is quite easy to make a parallel analysis of the multiple unit case based on the single unit case. In general, there are two classifications taken up in the literature on multiple unit auction. The first one is called the *discriminative* auction,

---

[135] Vickrey (1962).

[136] thus still retaining the symmetry assumption.

where the goods are awarded to the q highest bidders who in turn pay the amount that they bid. Thus, this is the multiple unit counterpart of the first-price sealed bid auction. As in the first price sealed bid, the $n - q$ losers in the auction come out with zero payoffs. The second type of multiple unit auction is called the *competitive* auction. Here, the q units of the good are awarded to the q highest bidders, but at a uniform price that is equal to the minimum successful bid. This is thus the counterpart of the second price sealed bid in the single unit case.[137] In this section, the independent values model will be discussed in general terms to provide a framework that characterizes the equilibrium prices in the two types of auctions.

The bidders are again assumed to have a utility function represented by

(73) $u_d = u(v_i - b_i)$ in the case of the discriminative auction

(74) $u_c = u(v_i - x)$ in the case of the competitive auction,

where

v_i is the valuation of the individual bidder i

b_i is the bid, which is also the price in the first-price sealed bid auction

x is the minimum successful bid

The minimum successful bid has a density function $f(x)$ in a discriminative auction and $g(x)$ in a competitive auction, such that the probability of winning a unit can be represented in the case of the discriminative auction, as

(75) $F(b) = \int_0^b f(x)dx$

which is the probability that a minimum successful bid is b or less.

It is also assumed that

(76) $F(b) \geq G(t) = \int_0^b g(x)dx$

---

[137] The term discriminative is adopted because the prices are variable across the bidders. On the othe hand, competitive is used to signify the similarity of the auction to the competitive market, where onl one price exists for all buyers.

114

for all b because the bidders will expect a lower bid under the discriminative than in a competitive auction.[138]

The expected utility of the bidder bidding for one unit of the good in the discriminative auction can be represented as

$$(77) \quad U_d = \int_0^b u(v_i - b_i) f(x) dx$$

and the FOC is

$$(78) \quad u(v_i - b_i^*) f(b_i^*) - u(v_i - b_i^*) F(b_i^*) = 0$$

The term $u(v_i - b_i) f(b_i)$ in the above equation can be recognized to be a decreasing function while the term $u(v_i - b_i) F(b_i)$ is an increasing function in the bid (or likewise in valuation) b. The optimal bid for a bidder in the discriminating auction is represented at the point b_i^* where the two functions cross.[139]

In the competitive auction, the expected utility of the individual is

$$(79) \quad U_c = \int_0^{b_i} u(v_i - x) g(x) dx$$

where $b_i \geq x$ if the bidder wins a unit of the good. The FOC is

$$(80) \quad u(v_i - p^*) g(p^*) = 0$$

A closer look at the equation will reveal that since the term $g(p^*) > 0$, the term $u(v_i - p^*)$ must be zero at the maximum payoff. But that will be the case when $p^* = v_i$, which means that the bidder bids his valuation, to maximize his chance of winning,

---

[138] This is the result of the dominant strategy in the second price sealed bid that we have already discussed in section 5.2.2, whereby each of the bidders bid the amount of their true willingness to pay, since the equilibrium price will be equal to the next highest bid. In the first price sealed bid, on the other hand, the bid is the price to be paid, such that the bidder will have to shade the bid to be able to capture some rent. Thus in general, the bid in the first price sealed bid auction is lower than in the second price sealed bid auction.

[139] One can recognize in these functions that when the bidder is risk neutral such that the marginal utility is a constant, then the second term is increasing because the probability of winning increases with increasing bids. The first term, on the other hand, shows that with a constant density f(x), the benefit from bidding high diminishes because the payment also increases.

since there is a positive probability that the equilibrium price to be paid is lower than his maximum willingness to pay, v_i.

5.6.2 The common value auction

As was discussed in section 5.5, the common value auction is a case when the valuation of the good is uncertain from the point of view of the bidder. One can then also talk of a discriminative multiple unit common value auction, and a competitive multiple unit common value auction. The main difference is only in as far as the representation of the density function $f(\cdot)$ and $g(\cdot)$, where now the joint density functions $f(x, v_i)$ and $g(x, v_i)$ are used to represent the effect of the uncertainty on the valuation v_i of bidder i. The expected utility of the bidder in a discriminating auction can be represented as

$$(81) \quad U_i = \int_0^\infty \int_0^{b_i} u(v_i - b_i) f(x, v_i) dx dv_i$$

The FOC is

$$(82) \quad \int_0^\infty u(v_i - b_i^*) f(b_i^*, v_i) dv_i - \int_0^\infty \int_0^{b_i^*} u'(v_i - b_i^*) f(x, v_i) dx dv_i$$

Again, the first term of the equation is a decreasing function of the bid, signifying a decreasing payoff because of the decrease in the rent capture with an increasing bid price, while the second term is an increasing function of the bid, signifying an increasing benefit from bidding high since the probability of winning increases.

For the competitive auction, the bidder's utility function can be represented by

$$(83) \quad U_c = \int_0^\infty \int_0^{p^*} u(v_i - x) g(x, v_i) dx dv_i$$

and the FOC is

$$(84) \quad \int_0^\infty u(v_i - p^*) g(p^*, v_i) dv_i = 0$$

and as in the independent value model, the joint density function $g(\cdot)$ is non-zero, making the optimal bid equal to the estimate of the valuation.

Thus, as in the independent values model, the bidder with the highest of all the estimates of the value of the good will win in both discriminative and competitive common value auctions.[140]

For an auction with risk neutral bidders, one can reformulate the FOC in equation (82) as

$$(85) \quad \int_0^\infty (v_i - b_i^*) f(b_i^*, v_i) dv_i - \int_0^\infty \int_0^{b_i^*} f(x, v_i) dx dv_i = 0$$

the second term of which can further be transformed to

$$(86) \quad f_1(b_i^*)\left[E_f(v_i|b_i^*) - b_i^*\right] = F_1(b_i^*)$$

being a cumulative marginal probability density function.[141]

Similarly, the FOC in equation (84), on the other hand can be written as

$$(87) \quad g_1(p^*)\left[E_g(v_i|p^*) - p^*\right] = 0$$

Since the expected equilibrium price in a discriminative auction cannot exceed that in the competitive auction, we have the condition:

$$(88) \quad E_f(v_i|b_i^*) \le E_g(v_i|p^*)$$

it can also be shown that

$$(89) \quad b_i^* = E_f(v_i|b_i^*) - \frac{F_1(b_i^*)}{f_1(b_i^*)} < E_f(v_i|b_i^*) \le E_g(v_i|p^*)$$

---

[140] However, as discussed in section 5.6, one is not free from the effects of the winner's curse.

[141] Note that $f(b_i^*, v_i) = f(v_i|b_i^*) f_1(b_i^*)$.

$E_f(v_i|b_i^*)$ is the price in the discriminative auction, while $E_g(v_i|p^*)$ is the price in the competitive auction. The equation verifies the statement that the equilibrium bid in the discriminative auction is lower than that in the competitive auction.

In the case where bidders are allowed to bid for more than one item, there are slight changes that one can introduce in the model. For instance, a maximum of k units may be bought by the bidders[142], such that $b_1 \le b_2 \le \cdots \le b_k$, Suppose $k = 2$. The expected payoff may be written as

$$(90) \quad U_d = \int_0^\infty \int_0^{b_1} u(kv_i - b_1 - b_2)f(x,v_i)dxdv_i + \int_0^\infty \int_{b_1}^{b_2} u((k-1)v_i - b_2)f(x,v_i)dxdv_i$$

where the first term involves the utility when both bids are accepted, while the second term involves the utility when only one bid (i.e., the highest bid) is accepted.

The FOC is

$$(90a) \quad \frac{\partial U_d}{\partial b_1} = \int_0^\infty u(2v_i - b_1^* - b_2^*)f(b_1^*,v_i)dv_i - \int_0^\infty \int_0^{b_1} u'(2v_i - b_1^* - b_2^*)f(x,v_i)dxdv_i$$

$$- \int_0^\infty u(v_i - b_2^*)f(b_1^*,v_i)dv_i = 0$$

and

$$(90b) \quad \frac{\partial U_d}{\partial b_2} = \int_0^\infty u(v_i - b_2^*)f(b_2^*,v_i)dv_i - \int_0^\infty \int_0^{b_1} u'(2v_i - b_1^* - b_2^*)f(x,v_i)dxdv_i$$

$$- \int_0^\infty \int_{b_1}^{b_2^*} u'(v_i - b_2^*)f(x,v_i)dxdv_i = 0$$

Given a risk neutral bidder, the FOC in equation (90a) can be rewritten as

$$(91a) \quad f_1(b_1^*)\left[E_f(v_i|b_1^*) - b_1^*\right] - F_1(b_1^*) = 0$$

and equation (90b) likewise as

---

[142] assuming the same expected valuation for the two goods.

(91b) $\quad f_1(b_2^*)\left[E_f(v_i|b_2^*) - b_2^*\right]F_1 - (b_2^*) = 0$

Since the estimates of the valuation for goods 1 and 2 are the same, the equations say that the risk neutral bidder should submit equal bids for both objects, at a price that is below the estimate, in order to shade the bids. This makes sense since this maximizes his chance of winning, while the payoff will be equal for both units of the good.[143]

In a competitive auction, the expected utility of the bidder can be represented as

$$(92) \quad U_c = \int_0^\infty \int_0^{b_1} u(kv_i - 2x)g(x, v_i)dxdv_i + \int_0^\infty \int_{b_1}^{b_2} u((k-1)v_i - x)g(x, v_i)dxdv_i$$

and the FOCs are

$$(93a) \quad \frac{\partial U_c}{\partial b_1} = \int_0^\infty u(2v_i - 2p_1^*)g(p_1^*, v_i)dv_i - \int_0^\infty u(v_i - p_1^*)g(p_1^*, v_i)dv_i = 0$$

and

$$(93b) \quad \frac{\partial U_c}{\partial b_2} = \int_0^\infty u(v_i - p_1^*)g(p_2^*, v_i)dv_i = 0$$

and for a risk-neutral bidder, the FOCs in equations (93a) and (93b)can be transformed into

$$(94a) \quad g(p_1^*)\left[E_g(v_i|p_1^*) - p_1^*\right] = 0$$

and

$$(94b) \quad g(p_2^*)\left[E_g(v_i|p_2^*) - p_2^*\right] = 0$$

which indicates that the risk neutral bidder bids up to his estimate of the expected value of the good, and as in the discriminative auction, the two bids are the same.

Again, this shows that the equilibrium bids in the competitive model of auctions allowing for multiple units to be bought will be at least equal to, and in the case of risk neutrality, may be higher than that in the discriminative auction.

---

[143] In contrast to the risk averse bidder, one bid should be higher than the other.

6. Auctions in privatization

6.1 Overview

In the previous chapter, it was attempted to discuss the general theoretical framework that forms the theory of auctioning. The various types of auctioning have been presented together with the equilibrium bids and payments, and the general results show that auctioning can be an efficient method of reallocating resources from one individual to the other, because the winner is always the one with the highest valuation.

In the specific case of privatization, it can be considered to be one of the most desirable methods to transfer the resources from the state to the private individuals. There are many reasons for this. First, as was already discussed, it can be desirable from the point of view of the privatizing state in as far as price setting is concerned. One of the biggest problems in privatization is to come up with an appropriate price by which to transfer the resource. Of course there are cases by which the resources are transferred at no cost to the recipient (in the case of mass privatization), especially when the government openly pronounces that it is not targeting any revenue for the transfer of the resource. As is shown in the theoretical section,– targeting efficiency -- in which case the person with the highest valuation wins—produces a by-product effect of maximum revenue. In the face of serious budgetary problems in the transforming economies, it is hardly understandable why additional revenues should be refused if this does not conflict with the main objective of achieving efficiency. Auctions provide a way by which the pricing problem faced by the government due to informational requirements is solved endogenously by the system or institution.

Second, since auctioning is a familiar method of resource transfer, it provides a simple mechanism that makes it easier for interested parties to verify any of the rules and regulations that apply in the course of the bidding process. In other words, auctions can provide a very transparent resource transfer mechanism that prevents many of the problems faced in privatization programs, such as corruption and insecure property rights, which then enhances the speed and effectiveness of the privatization process. It prevents the politicians from having a hand in the transfer of the resource to a privileged few, unless they are willing to risk their positions and privileges as public servants. But certainly the most important outcome of all is the fact that the politicians do not have to search for ways to find out the most efficient use of the resource. As shown, auctioning achieves efficiency by promoting competition between bidders which lead them to reveal the information that the government in the first place needed to know if they themselves, in the case of state ownership and governance, would like to lead the economic activities to the condition that use the resource in question efficiently.

In most auction literature, the objective set up by the principal (the government) is to maximize revenue. Some might argue that there is in fact no net benefit in having revenue generation as an objective, because auctioning only provides a way of reallocating the resource, not any increase in net social welfare. The reason for this is that the revenue is a mere transfer payment from the private individual within the domestic economy to the state, thus involving no increase in the social welfare of the economy in general. This is however, not necessarily true, especially in the case when the resource is transferred to the one who will use it in the most efficient manner. The mere transfer of the resource to such individuals is therefore welfare-increasing, but the way it is implemented supports an objective of revenue maximization, which is in principle not harmful to the citizenry. In addition, the winners in the auctioning process are those who normally have the financial resources to support their bids. In this case, the gains from the transfer of the resource are not simply washed out; the financial resource is also put into a more productive use via the investment in the purchase of the resource.

6.2 The P-A problem revisited

To provide a unifying structure on the theoretical discussions presented in chapters 4 and 5, this section reviews the basic findings to show that auction design is indeed a principal-agent problem which may be very useful for solving the problems of privatization in general, and of land in particular.

Recalling the discussion that the official pronouncements of the government for the major reason for privatization could be a variety of factors like efficiency, revenue generation, competition, income redistribution, employment generation, proper distribution of risk, and equity, it is actually possible to summarize this by saying that the main objective is to raise the social welfare of the individuals in the society, by transferring the resource possessed by the state. However, the mere transfer of the resource that achieves any or perhaps all of these pronounced objectives is basically not easy in the world of asymmetric information. That is, the government does not possess the information it needs in order to implement a transfer of the property rights that is consistent with its objective. The information is more often than not, possessed as private information of individuals who are interested to acquire the resource and use it in a specific economic activity. In the words of Rasmusen (1990), the government, which is the principal, has the coarser information set, while the agent has the finer information set, which gives the latter some sort of an advantage. The government is faced with a variety of mechanisms it could implement in order to provide incentives to the agents to reveal the relevant information so that the objective can be achieved. But as long as the privacy of information is respected, then coercion is in principle not an option for the government to use. The private information must be revealed voluntarily. The mechanism that the government should implement has the character of ex ante efficiency, that is, on the average, the mechanism is implementable (that it is acceptable to the participating agents, or in what amounts to the same thing, it satisfies the participation constraint of the agents) even before any message is revealed by the agents about their private information, and that the agents have, on the average, higher payoffs by sending a message that is positively correlated to the information that they have that is relevant to the principal.

In the discussion on the auction theory, it was established that the process can be information revealing for the principal, and the result can in general be efficient given the proper design parameters. For a privatizing agency, the information requirements to achieve the efficiency, compared to other mechanisms such as private negotiations, is minimal because the agents reveal voluntarily the information necessary. This is a desirable characteristic, because then a privatizing agency need not expend resources just to be able to collect the information needed to transfer the resource it owns following certain objectives. Thus, apart from the direct gain by allocating the resource to the one who values it most, the government saves some of its resources that would have otherwise been spent for information collection or monitoring.

If indeed auctioning is a superior method to use in privatization, then it may be reasonable to imagine that it will be more generally implemented in transition economies than otherwise. In the following section, a discussion on the recent experiences in the use of auctions for general privatization as well as in transition economies will be presented, and hopefully a general assessment of the belief of policymakers towards its advantages can be evaluated against some apparent results so far achieved.

6.3 Recent experiences.

6.3.1 Small scale auctioning

Most literature in auctioning in transforming economies reveal that auctions are implemented as a mechanism to privatize only small scale and some medium scale enterprises.[144] Rondinelli (1995) for instance identifies via his survey of methods of privatization that auctioning is typically used as a means to transfer the ownership of the small businesses which cannot be restituted to the former owners. Although he claims that it is so far the best means to rapidly privatize the very large numbers of small service and retail business in Central and Eastern European countries, and in addition generates revenues for the local governments, Chilosi (1995) claims that in practice, auctioning has implemented privatization at a slow pace and that the financial results from auctioning has given only a small contribution to the revenues of the privatizing government. Why Chilosi made such a conclusion has to be examined in relation to the country which is privatizing. In his paper, he focused on the privatization via auctioning in the Russian Federation, which has implemented the first pilot program in 1992 with the assistance of the International Monetary Fund (IMF). In this pilot project, a total of 20-25 properties were sold each week (totaling 37,000 by the beginning of 1993). However, specifically in Russia, there was a tendency to prefer rather management or employee buy-outs than auctioning. This might be explained by the rampant corruption that has plagued the Russian privatization program; a mechanism of auctioning would in general be transparent if correctly implemented. Naturally, if the information on the schedules of auctions is not properly dispersed, then it is to be expected that partiality of the privatizing officials can enter the process, leading to low revenues and perhaps inefficiency. In general, therefore, the reluctance to implement auction and the rampant corruption of the state officials

---

[144] See Rondinelli (1995), Clarke(1994) , Chilosi (1995) among others.

have been rather the main reason why privatization of the small enterprises produced modest revenues.

Similarly, the Czech Republic has issued a "Small Privatization Law" which allowed the privatization of some 100,000 units of small state-owned enterprises via the sale to private individuals, in the first round to local nationals and in the second round to all other interested investors.

Clarke also claims that there may be some potential problems in general in the use of auctioning, because it assumes a perfect financial market.[145] However, this is not really a valid claim. While it is true that the financial markets of the transforming economies are also still at the stage of development to provide support to large investments in capital assets, a payment scheme can be developed in order to ease this problem. The fact that many of the countries have adopted it so far as a mechanism to quickly implement the resource transfer is a good indication of the relative administrative ease by which it can be designed and implemented in order to support the private sector development. How much revenue is collected and whether efficiency is achieved depends on the commitment of the privatizing agency to implement a truly competitive auction.

In other countries, such as in Chile, auctions also found their way through the system of successfully privatizing not just small enterprises in the 1970's and 1980's, but also large-scale enterprises. However, there is hardly any analysis done on these small scale auctions, and it is not possible to make a definitive statement of their general effectiveness in the practice of a privatization.

6.3.2 Large Scale

One of the biggest success stories in the design of auction mechanism for privatizing large scale state assets is the sale of spectrum rights[146] in the United States via auction, which begun in December 1994. It was considered as a breakthrough by many economists[147] because prior to the December auction, the spectrum licenses were

---

[145] He makes a stronger statement by saying that it is unsuitable for large scale privatization.

[146] Radio communications spectrum licenses to be used for wireless communication services called personal communication services (PCS) for telephones, data communication devices, faxes, pagers, inter-active home videos, among others.

[147] Milgrom (1998).

awarded either via direct assignment by the regulators to firms believed to be able to use the license best, or through simple lotteries to those who are interested to acquire it. The first expectedly involved a lot of work for the administrators in terms of information collection, and was thus very slow in terms of asset transfer. This has caused fears that the communications industry development would lag behind considerably compared to other countries. The second is similar to the mass privatization that is seen in many transforming economies, simply giving away the asset with substantial values, which later on can be sold in the market. The common thing in the two privatization procedures is the loss in resources in the implementation process in terms of the time, efforts and financial resources of the government to get the mechanism through, and the loss in terms of rent-seeking behavior of the implementers, which has led to conditions of inefficiency.[148]

Even when there was a breakthrough in the government's decision to use auction to privatize its spectrum licenses, there was work to be done on the rules that govern the actual bidding process to be adopted. For this, they needed to look at what theory says about efficiency results in various auction procedures, considering the strategic behavior of the bidders given the rules set up. In addition, they needed to look around for some related experiences in auctioning of large scale assets, preferably also in spectrum auctions, if it existed. At the time, there were two relevant auction designs which later on proved to be embarrassing to the implementing government, that in New Zealand in 1990 and the other one in Australia in 1992.[149]

From the two large-scale auctions, it was apparent that the design of the rules of the auctions does matter. In New Zealand, a second-price sealed bid auction was adopted for the separate units of the licenses, on the basis of the theoretical analysis in the Vickrey auctions. However, this was clearly a wrong approach, as later on proved to be, because with such multiple units of licenses, the approach should have been like the one presented in the discussion on competitive auction in section 5.7, where the accepted bids have to pay a uniform price equal to the highest rejected bid. In addition, the choice of a simultaneous sealed bid tender proved to be damaging to the results of

---

[148] One may argue that this is not so bad as long as there is a secondary market where the asset can be bought and sold. This is true, but then the gains accrue only to the awardees, which in principle should have been received by the government. As Milgrom (1998) said, the winners got some revenues by selling the license to legitimate telephone companies who actually needed the licenses, thereby generating some costs in the production of the communication service. However, no corresponding revenue came in to the coffers of the government.

[149] See McAfee and McMillan (1996) and McMillan (1994) for an analysis of the spectrum auction.

the auction because the bidders faced a complicated problem of how many and how much to bid, thus forcing them to bid for more units than necessary just to insure themselves against the risk of losing.

Because the auction process is transparent to the public, it was easy to verify what had actually been bid, and what had been paid for by the winning bidders. In many of the bids for nationwide UHF lots, the winning bidders paid about 20% of their actual bid; but there were cases like the winning bidder bid NZ$100,000 but paid only NZ$6, or another with a bid of NZ$7.0 million and paid only NZ$5,000.

The case in Australia was similar. However, the government used the first-price sealed bid auction, where deposits were not required to participate in the auction, no restriction on multiple bids (for an object), and no default penalty. Failure of a winner to pay within a specified period means that the second highest bidder wins, who is again given a grace period by which to pay; the process goes on until an awardee is able to pay within the prescribed period. It turned out that bidders have submitted multiple bids for each object, such that in many cases, the first several highest bids come from the same company. Of course, upon knowing that this is the case, the company has no incentive to pay the amount of the highest bid. It will wait until the first several high bids are disqualified, because no penalty is imposed. That was exactly what happened, and the government spent so much time and effort in awarding and re-awarding the bids. In the meantime, the winning bidder scouted around for potential buyers. The first license was sold for A$117 million and immediately resold for a A$21 million profit.

From this, the designers of the US spectrum auction learned quite a lot, and decided for a simultaneous, multiple unit auction with several pre-scheduled rounds of ascending bidding. This auction design allows the bidders to collect information during the bidding process and renew their bids or bidding strategies according to the new information. It also allowed the bidders to combine and replace licenses depending on their standing in the current bidding stage. The auction was a complicated open bidding which was different from the standard English since it used the computer technology to support the process of information management - - thereby not needing the actual presence of bidders for the submission of their bids. The design process treated the auction as a common value auction. It respected the fact that only the bidders will know exactly how they can use and combine the local and nationwide licenses to serve their business interests - - an information that is not easily available to the government. The auction allowed for cases where the bidders can evaluate potential synergetic combinations (where they can have some economies of scale) and potential substitutes, on the basis of their business projections. Penalties for bid withdrawals were imposed.

In the first set of auction on narrowband licenses, the government expected to collect only about US$50 million, but the total revenue collected from the sale after a week of bidding was $617 million, a substantial increase from what has been initially expected. In the succeeding auctions, it proved to be that the auction design promoted technical efficiency. The biggest of all the series of auctions raised the government a total of US$8.0 billion in revenues. The winning bidders were also satisfied with the process. These all were good indications of the success of the large-scale auction ever.

The experience in the U.S. spectrum auctions proved that indeed, the usefulness of auctions is not just limited to an academic exercise among auction theorists. It has wide-reaching implications in helping reallocate resources where problems in pricing are inherent because of the lack of information from the buyers. The seller need not have the information on how the various different units of the asset could be combined to produce various other goods and services that would benefit the consumers and the society in general. In other words, it is a method by which the market process dominates and determines the outcome. In particular, McAffee and McMillan (1996) have indicated that the simultaneous ascending auction is an effective mechanism for selling multiple units of interdependent items, whether they are complements or substitutes.

Unfortunately, no similar case of large scale privatization via auctioning can be found in the transition economies. This has something to do with the fact that the experience in the US was really a novelty; a jump from the traditional skepticism and perhaps also suspect by practitioners on the use of auctions. Even at the beginning, the dominance of game theorists in the design of the spectrum auctions was considered by some critics (such as the Economist) as "letting the lunatics" into the process, introducing incomprehensible game-theoretic terms like backward induction, sub-game perfect equilibrium, among others, in the analysis of the behavior of the bidders. Until enough positive experience is gained via the use of auctions, it might still be something very much distrusted by the more practical policy-makers.

6.4 Auction for privatizing land

6.4.1 Experiences

In the survey of the various different methods used for privatization, it is clear that there is indeed a general bias against the use of auctions for privatization. For small scale enterprises, it proved to accommodate inefficiencies in the transforming economies, even though the theory predicts otherwise. But as was already discussed in the previous section, the result depends on the design of the auction given the characteristics of the good to be reallocated, as well as the genuine commitment of the privatizing institution to adopt a truly competitive and transparent mechanism.

In any case, the data shows that most of the countries have mainly firstly adopted the policy of restitution of the land to the former owners, and then protected the tenancy rights of the farm members and workers who are still working on the current farms.[150] Referring again to table 1 in section 2.5.6, there is still a considerable amount of land to be privatized even after having implemented the two major policies of privatization. In most countries, this will have to involve other forms of resource transfer. However, there is very little indication that any of these countries seek to adopt a mechanism of auctioning. The agriculture sector is traditionally a powerful lobby group which always enjoyed protection from its government. This makes it difficult to implement path-breaking policies that may also dislodge the traditional influential blocks in the sector. Agricultural land is a highly political good, and most politicians have their hands off from the issue, before they burn themselves. To date, there is no substantive data that show any form of an auction mechanism for land in any of the transforming economies of East and Central Europe.[151] In the former East Germany, a total of about 1.3 million hectares of land is to be privatized via a mechanism that can be characterized as a mixture of sealed bid auction and direct negotiations. Sealed bid auction in the

---

[150] See Csaki and Lerman (1996) p.238.

[151] There is, however, one very small auction of land conducted in China, as reported by a television news agency which the author missed to see. In this sell-off, the local government has organized an English auction of the several land units that the government owns. Naturally, only the local farmers came to the event, ready to bid in order to acquire the land. It proved to be also a disaster, since many of the rules of the auctions were taken for granted by the designers of the event, leading to confusion on the part of the poor farmers. There were instances when the farmers bid way over their capacity to pay for the land (some sort of a winner's curse), their bidding behavior mainly being driven by the atmosphere in the auction hall. In the end, one farmer needed to work outside agriculture in order to earn the money to pay for the land.

sense that the bidders have to submit a bid for the land and the assets tied with it, plus a management plan which is then to be evaluated by the central privatizing agency, after which some negotiations with the prospective candidate will be undertaken. The winner will be the one judged to have the best management plan.[152] One can just imagine how long and at what cost to the government the whole process will take before it reached its conclusion.[153]

6.4.2 Potentials

Given the experience so far of the US in the spectrum auction, it is reasonable to believe that such a success is also possible to happen in the reallocation of agricultural land. There are similarities in the sense that agricultural land is also bought mainly for its use as a productive resource which brings profits to the firm. The value of the land therefore depends on the foreseen use - - which is private information to the bidders. Land units can also be combined in various forms to support a vertical or horizontal integration of farm activities that increase the profitability of the land; it can also have possible substitutes, be it perfect or imperfect. These information will be extremely difficult and costly for the government to collect, and even if they require such information to be submitted by the bidders, it will still entail large amounts of administrative time and effort to verify the information that is contained in the plans of the agricultural businesses, as is the case in East Germany.[154]

The main requirement, it seems, is political determination and courage to set up a transparent, and market-oriented mechanism to privatize the land. The results need not be embarrassing to the implementing agency if the proper design of the rules of the auctions in relation to bidder behavior is considered. Since the agriculture sector is, in many of these countries, a big source of domestic income and employment, a rapid privatization that encourages efficiency and at the same time generates revenue for the

---

[152] see section 2.5.5 for a discussion on the East German scheme of land privatization.

[153] Apart from this, the restrictions posed by the German government make it unprofitable for all qualified buyers to acquire the land. For instance, as a long-term lessee, it is far better to keep the contract as it is than buy the land. For most of them, it is rather better to wait for the chance that they have accumulated enough capital to purchase the land, than to immediately buy at the current conditions. The situation is not better for the non-lessee. On the whole, this has now been reflected in far less demand for land purchase than the government has expected. See Schönberg (1997).

[154] besides, the sell off system adopted in Germany is very inflexible, effectively putting barriers to the determined farmers to look for alternatives in case they lose a chance on one land they bid on. This can be very tiring for them, especially if they face uncertainty as to the rest of the available lands that will be sold off.

local government is a very positive factor for the growth of the economy. The unconditional transfer of property rights upon sale relieves the government of the burden of unnecessary monitoring until the end of the moratorium normally imposed by the various transforming economies on the use of the land as well as the eventual resale, if the owner decides to do so. Property rights are cleared faster, and the farmers can rather plan their production activities better. Financial support for its long-term activity also becomes easier to secure because the land and the assets attached to it can be a very good form of security.[155] Such a market-based transfer of the resource is one of the most effective ways by which the agricultural sector development can be accelerated in many of these transforming economies.

6.4.3 Is auctioning equitable?

One of the biggest concerns in the issue of privatization is equity, and the situation in the land market is not an exception. Sappington and Stiglitz (1987) refer to the equity aspects of privatization as the desire of the government to fulfill certain distributional objectives, in agreement to the discussion presented in the section of equity issues of privatization in chapter 2. In essence, when one searches for a method of privatization, one of the main criteria to fulfill is the desirable redistribution of wealth and/or resources. In particular, the privatization must not permit a worsening of the distribution of wealth within the society.

One of the main advantages of auction is its non-discretionary nature. Once the rules of the auctions have been established, the privatizing agency has a relatively small scope for discretionary moves that benefits some favored individuals. As long as the information on the rules and regulations governing the auction procedure is well spread and each individual has an equal access to the auction, then one can say that auctioning is ex ante equitable. It gives a fair chance to everyone to participate in the process and gain in the event he is awarded the asset privatized, thus contributing positively to income redistribution. However, auctioning is not the only privatization method that can be considered non-discretionary. In principle, lottery achieves the most non-discretionary and thus equitable redistribution of the resource ex ante. The

---

[155] A bank will have no use of a security that cannot be sold in the market. Moratoria are thus simply barriers that increase the cost to the farmer of acquiring the asset.

other method that is also non-discretionary and ex ante equitable is employee or mass privatization. However, there are clear ex post differences between these methods.

In employee or mass privatization schemes, only a selected few benefit from the privatization. In particular, only the employees directly working for the enterprise to be privatized receive the vouchers/shares that increases their wealth immediately after the privatization. Citizens who are working in public service do not have this privilege nor do they have any chance to increase their wealth as a result of the privatization process. To the extent that the government does not receive any revenue from the transfer of the resource ownership, there is also no room for the government to provide improved services to the non-beneficiaries of the mass privatization to increase their welfare level. In this case, mass privatization is non discretionary, but not totally equitable ex ante. Lottery, on the other hand, is equitable ex ante. It provides equal chance to all in acquiring the state assets. In both cases, however, there could be some form of inequalities ex-post. The small, risk averse individuals who have been awarded shares of the assets will in general not find it attractive enough to keep the shares. Firstly, these shares are risky since their values depend on the performance of the enterprises. Even if, as employees, they have some information about the performance of the enterprise, their own efforts towards improving the profitability may be too small in relation to the whole company that there is no significant effect in exerting the effort to make sure that it is worth keeping the shares. Wealthy individuals, on the other hand, are much less risk averse, and even if they have not too much information about the company, they could find it worthwhile to hold on to the shares, and even buy some of them from the poorer individuals. This way, the wealthy are able to exercise full rent extraction, which gives them the highest advantage in the scheme of privatization implemented. Besides, such a situation also leads to an even higher concentration of wealth, considering that the wealthy have comparatively stronger bargaining power than the small, poor average individuals in trading the shares.

Some arguments can be raised about the fact that only wealthy individuals, or people who have access to financial resources, have the privilege to participate in the auction. In the context of the transforming economies, these will be the people who have been able to accumulate wealth during the old regime. However, under the principles of democracy now embraced by these economies, direct appropriations of these wealth is not anymore possible. Thus, an argument of making them pay for the resource at the highest possible price is one way by which a desirable redistribution of wealth can be accomplished. For this reason, auction is ex post equitable and in many ways superior to the other non-discretionary methods of privatization.

It is also important to note that most of the privatization methods that establish secure property rights that allow trading and exchange could potentially lead to patterns of ownership that are efficient, provided that bargaining costs are low and there are no externalities.[156] Under this argument, then it should not matter which privatization method is used, because as long as secure property rights result from the privatization process, the market will lead itself to an efficient level. Bringing in the issue of equity, however, makes it necessary to eliminate or to reduce to a minimum the discretion of the privatizing agency to award the assets to those it favors. This also reduces problems in rent-seeking that eventually enrich only the framers and implementers of the privatization process, without the rest of the society benefiting from it. Besides, in the real world where other non-participants are also affected by the trading activity, not every trade can be value-increasing. Efficiency cannot be guaranteed even if property rights have been clearly defined. In this case, there is a clear advantage to assigning the property rights to the asset to the individual who puts the highest value to its ownership and/or use. Auctioning is therefore superior compared to most forms of privatization methods in the sense that it awards the resource to those who value it most. To quote Maskin (1992, p.115) on the use of auction: "Privatizing productive assets in formerly centralized economies is a task to which auctions seem especially well suited."

---

[156] See Coase (1960).

7. Modeling an auction mechanism for land

7.1 Design considerations

For the agriculture sector in general, the process of transformation involves the two inseparable issues of land privatization and farm restructuring. This means that, although admittedly, the task of designing a privatization process is difficult, the foremost criteria that most of the transforming economies need to address is a transfer of ownership and its corresponding assets that leads the market closer to efficiency, if not at the most efficient level, coupled by the creation of a market process that promotes competition and dynamic adjustment in the farming sector. This is important in, as well as after the privatization process, for these countries have an agriculture sector that employs the major share of the total labor force (Csaki and Lerman, 1996). This means that, as in the case observed in many developing countries, the development in the sector has a strong bearing consequences in the development of the economy.

The discussion in the previous chapters have all tried to build up the case that one of the best ways to implement such a privatization scheme is via auctioning. This chapter will attempt to show this analytically. In addition, some discussion on the key factors that influence the outcome of the process will be addressed, in order to put together some general guidelines on how an optimal auction for land can be implemented.

7.1.1 Principal-agent problems in land privatization.

Chapters 4 and 6 have discussed the agency theory and its application in the problem of privatization. It was pointed out that privatization in general is a solution to the P-A problem characterizing the inefficiency in a system of central planning. In the case of the now transforming economies, the inefficiency comes from a system where the residual rights still belong to the state such that the agents do not have the incentive to perform an effort level that is consistent with their true abilities. [157] In the agricultural sector where land is one of the most important assets of use, the transfer of the residual

---

[157] Or more generally, that resources are not used up to their full productivity levels.

rights to private individuals is the key to a long-term agricultural development process. However, that is only a first step; a freely operating market for land is another requirement to allow adjustments in farm structures that promote efficiency of the farms. In both cases, the government is at a disadvantage in the sense of not having enough information on the true productivity of the land as a resource. At best, it can only encourage private individuals to share this information so that the appropriate allocation of land can be identified.

The principal-agent problem in land privatization can thus be summarized as follows. There is a state who is in possession of land (and assets attached to it) who would like to maximize his utility by transferring the ownership of the land to private individuals. However, if the utility of the state is represented by the sum of the producers' and consumers' surplus, then the mere transfer of the ownership to private individuals will not be sufficient to guarantee a maximum utility. A transfer is already a Pareto-improvement since in the process, the residual rights are transferred to private individuals. However, in addition, the outcome of the allocation must be such, that the land units are allocated to the individual or firm who is most efficient in using the resource as a productive asset. In a world of imperfect information, this is equivalent to saying that the individual with the highest expected valuation should acquire the resource. Following the previous discussions on the theory of auction, it will be sufficient to represent the utility of the state as the revenue from the sell off process, since the outcome achieves efficiency, given the appropriate design of the auction rules. In addition, the proceeds can be used to provide public goods to consumers, thus generating consumer surplus.

The principal, which is the state, maximizes the expected revenue from the auction of the land units subject to two constraints: the individual rationality constraint (or participation constraint) and the incentive compatibility constraint. The first indicates that the participating bidders should expect to be at least as well off as before if they decide to participate in the auction. The second says that the participating bidders should have an incentive to reveal their true valuation for the land, that is, that the bids should appropriately represent the valuation that they have on the land, such that the higher their valuation, the higher will be the bid. This applies to both cases when the valuation is independent private or common.

7.1.2 Informational Requirements

There are many different concerns on the part of policy-makers regarding the privatization of land. Chapter 2 has discussed the major issues surrounding the political, social and other institutional problems. For instance, the reluctance to implement a truly democratic privatization process rests on the concern that too much private sector freedom will produce monopolistic structures that allow the new land owners to capture too much economic rent that in the end curtails production efficiency. In this case, there is an attempt for the government to collect as much information as possible on the productive efficiency of the land units to be able to judge whether an individual or a firm will be in a position to really use the resource efficiently, in accordance with the social objectives. However, the reality of the situation is that, the government can never be better informed compared to private individuals, nor can it even strive to be equally informed about the best use of the resource. Therefore, attempts at establishing institutions to ensure that the new owners will be honest as to their planned resource use will be a costly exercise to undertake, whereas it nowhere guarantees that it will achieve more efficiency. In any case, ex post, it will be a matter of long and painstaking juridical process to justify taking away land that has been erroneously transferred to the less efficient individual. The same mistakes can be realized the next time when the government must once more identify the individual who will use the resource better. The process will have no end. The government has a higher probability of making such identification errors than any other individual who is interested in the land, simply because the latter will always be better informed. On the other hand, schemes like mass privatization do not guarantee the absence of monopolistic structures ex post. Recall the discussion in chapter 6 that although this scheme may appear to be non-discriminatory and highly egalitarian, investors can still buy the shares at depressed prices especially when they have the greater bargaining power and that the holders of the shares are highly risk averse. Land concentration can still occur under these circumstances.

Thus, a process that transfers the land requiring the minimum information from the prospective owners will be the most efficient institutional form of a privatization process.[158] Any other form of restriction on the use and disposal ex post transfer will be inefficient in the sense of preventing the market to adjust to a point of efficiency.

---

[158] This is consistent with Hurwicz (1972) theorem of informational efficiency.

Auctioning has been shown to have asymptotic optimality properties[159] which then approximates the competitive solution, moving the market closer to efficiency.

7.1.3 Pricing Problems

The pricing problem faced by the privatizing agency is related to the uncertainty of information about the factors that affect the price of the land. At best, the government can make some estimates of the value of the land unit to be sold given some indicators, like quality of soil, farm type, accessibility, etc. However, there are an infinite number of possible combinations of all these factors that affect the valuation, and the estimate of the government on the potential value of the land, as previously mentioned, will never be superior compared to that of the interested bidders, especially if synergies or external effects are present. If external effects are present, then it will be even more of an informational burden to the state to identify which combinations will produce the maximum benefit to the society, considering all conditions in the factor and output markets. As this information is a result of an estimation process that requires careful prognosis not only of the physical factors that affect the production process, but also of the market conditions, it is not necessarily Pareto-improving for the government to dictate the resource use it has judged to be best, nor is it in a better position to judge that a particular proposed resource use by any farm is inferior. Auctions, as has been shown, are the best form of resource transfer that takes away the problems of setting up the right prices. And if the Hayek (1945) hypothesis is considered, the price that the resource has fetched in the market should already reflect all the possible information that is needed to fulfill an efficient allocation of the resource. In other words, selling the land to the one with the highest offer ensures economic efficiency, which as is standard even in neo classical economics, is welfare-improving.

---

[159] That is, as the number of participants increases, the closer is the price of the good in the market to the true valuation, and thus the lower will be the economic rent gained by the agent. See Milgron (1979).

7.2 Multiple-unit auction of land.

7.2.1 General features

7.2.1.1 Multiple unit common value

Following the discussion in section 5.7.2, it is by now clear that the privatization of land can be modeled as a common value auction with multiple units. This is because although there may be one objective value for any unit of land to be sold, no single individual will possess perfect information about the factors that influence the true value, and therefore no single individual, not even the principal, will know for sure what the value of the unit(s) of land would be. This modeling process takes into consideration the variability arising from the information collected that forms the estimates of the quality of land and its first-best productive use, as well as the variability that comes from information in forming estimates of the factor and output prices, which also eventually enter the estimate of the true value of the land to the farmer.

7.2.1.2 Synergetic effects

Owing to the fact that land is a fixed productive asset, one can follow the simple optimality principle that given the estimates of output and factor prices, there is one optimal combination of factors that maximizes the farmer's profit. The higher the profit expected from the use of the land, the higher is the value of the land to the farmer. If the resource land is additively separable, then one can simply add the economic rent accruing to every single unit of land used in the production process. Effectively, in auctions, this amounts to a common value auction with multiple, independent units of land for which a separate bid can be tendered by the bidders. The modeling process used in section 5.7.2 therefore applies.

Complications come in when one assumes the presence of synergetic effects in the use of land. In particular, this will be the case when some bidders have collected information that some land combinations will produce external economies that makes the unit value of combined land higher than when they are used separately. In agricultural production, this may be the cases when horizontal or vertical integration provides the opportunity for the farmer to increase the profitability of the farm business, thereby increasing the economic value of the land to them. Whereas there are farmers who see the potentials of integration, there are also some farmers who have only the information on one particular unit of land, that is, they are interested only in one unit of land. Thus, this modeling process considers the heterogeneity of the information collected by the bidders on the land in question, but also considers differences in preferences which is then reflected on the variation in the estimates of the unit value of the land.

7.2.2 Simultaneous vs. sequential auction

It has been established that in general, simultaneous auctioning is superior to sequential auctioning[160] when there are external effects.[161] This is because such an auction procedure gives the opportunity to the bidders to incorporate the synergy effects into their bids. The effect is actually an improvement in the efficiency results of the sell off process. In contrast, sequential auction induces strategic bidding situations that lead to inefficiency results.

In view of the problems faced in transforming economies, a fully simultaneous auction may not be possible to implement. The government is still facing identification problems as to the parcel of lands that could be sold. It is not unusual that cadastral surveys are still missing, and information on the total available land may not be known. However, instead of a government that invests its resources on trying to set up control mechanisms and institutions that would collect more information than is required in the auction to establish the first best use of the land, it may very well be better off collecting information on the available land it has to privatize. In some cases, such as in East Germany, a considerable amount of land has been leased out to private individuals. This means that these lands have already been practically identified; otherwise a lease contract will not be possible to make. In this case, the major activity of the BVVG must be to collect all the data on the available transferable land. A simultaneous auction can therefore be adopted.

In many countries, there is naturally a trade-off between postponing the auction all together until the time that all parcels of land have been duly identified to adopt a simultaneous auction that promotes efficient allocation of land, and the immediate transfer of the property rights in order to change the incentive structure of the

---

[160] Sequential is awarding the resource one unit after another.

[161] See McAffe and McMillan (1996), and Krishna and Rosenthal (1997) for more details.

agricultural production process. In the latter, it is important for the identified agricultural lands to be privatized as soon as possible, simply because there are immediate gains in terms of productive efficiency from the mere transfer of the residual rights to private individuals. This means that there is also an advantage to auctioning off identified land units with no legal problems ahead of those which have not yet been identified, and ahead of those already identified but with existing legal problems in transferring the ownership. This process would then be very similar to a sequential auction in relation to the total potential transferable land, but simultaneous in relation to the total freely transferable identified lands. Individuals who have already acquired land in the first rounds of the auction will have informational as well as technical advantage over those who did not acquire land previously. Depending on the price settled in the previous auction[162] this could drive some of the bidders out of the bidding process, which then reduces the degree of competition (as the number of participants decreases). The strategic behavior of the bidders thus changes. In particular, the bids will generally be low, producing a low revenue for the state. Although the reader is made aware of this problem, it is beyond the scope of this research to dwell on the administrative aspects surrounding the immediate identification of the land units to be privatized. It is rather assumed then, that it will be possible to adopt a simultaneous auction procedure on the basis of a fixed supply of properly identified and documented units of land, however heterogeneous this collection of land units may seem from the point of view of the privatizing agency. The following analysis will proceed on the basis of this assumption.

Because of the extremely complicated nature of such a modeling process, the analysis will be based on a two-bidder type model, a local bidder who is interested in only one unit of land, and a combinatorial bidder who is interested in several units of land because his information set reflects a synergetic effect in the case when the units of land are combined in the production process. The notation used in section 5.7.2 is adopted in the following analysis.

The basic framework of the model can be summarized as follows. A discriminatory bid is firstly analyzed. There are two types of bidders, one is interested only on a single unit (a local bidder) and the other is interested in both units. The local bidder's valuation for a single unit is to be indicated as v_l, while the other as v_j. Bidder j

---

[162] which sends a signal to the next auction.

estimates that the total value of having both units of land is $2\beta v$, where $\beta > 1$ is the positive external effect on the profitability of the farm. That is, having both units is worth more per unit than the sum of the two units of land. As before, there is a joint density function for the estimates of the value of the land, $f(\cdot)$ with a corresponding distribution function $F(\cdot)$.

It is also assumed that the combinatorial bidders are interested to acquire only two units of land, and the units of land have identical valuations when treated separately. The expected payoff of a combinatorial bidder can be derived from equation (90) of chapter 5:

$$(1)\ U_j = \int_0^\infty \int_0^{b_1} u(k\beta v_j - b_1 - b_2) f(x, v_j)\, dx\, dv_j + \int_0^\infty \int_{b_1}^{b_2} u((k-1)v_j - b_2) f(x, v_j)\, dx\, dv_j$$

where as before, $k = 2$ is the number of units of land. $\beta > 1$ is the external effect.

The expected payoff of a local bidder can be reformulated from equation (81) of chapter 5:

$$(2)\quad U_i = \int_0^\infty \int_0^{b_i} u(v_i - b_i) f(x, v_i)\, dx\, dv_i$$

It is also worth noting that the distinction of the local from the combinatorial bidders has relevance in the actual policy on land privatization. In Germany, for instance, there is a policy that only the local farmers can bid for land. To the extent that other units of land are spatially located somewhere else, but still provide positive externalities in combining with a local unit of land, then it will be in principle be difficult to take advantage of the benefits resulting from the synergy. The discussion on effects of such a policy appears at the end of this subsection.

The FOCs for the combinatorial bidder are

$$(3) \quad \frac{\partial U_j}{\partial b_1} = \int_0^\infty u(2\beta v_j - b_1^* - b_2^*)f(b_1^*, v_j)dv_{ji}$$

$$- \int_0^\infty \int_0^{b_1} u'(2\beta v_j - b_1^* - b_2^*)f(x, v_j)dxdv_j$$

$$- \int_0^\infty u(v_j - b_2^*)f(b_1^*, v_j)dv_j = 0$$

and

$$(4) \quad \frac{\partial U_j}{\partial b_2} = \int_0^\infty u(v_j - b_2^*)f(b_2^*, v_j)dv_j - \int_0^\infty \int_0^{b_1} u'(2\beta v_j - b_1^* - b_2^*)f(x, v_j)dxdv_j$$

$$- \int_0^\infty \int_{b_1}^{b_2^*} u'(v_j - b_2^*)f(x, v_j)dxdv_j = 0$$

and as before, the FOC of a local bidder is

$$(5) \quad \int_0^\infty u(v_i - b_i^*)f(b_i^*, v_i)dv_i - \int_0^\infty \int_0^{b_i^*} u'(v_i - b_i^*)f(x, v_i)dxdv_i$$

The result is much the same as the analysis in section 5.7.2, that is, in the case when the combinatorial bidder is risk neutral, the Nash equilibrium should be that of submitting equal bids for the two units of land at the price lower than the mean of the density of the estimated value of the good.

To help simplify the analysis, it may be useful to adopt the analysis appearing in Rosenthal and Wang (1997):

Suppose the bidders are risk averse, and there are n local bidders and m combinatorial bidders. Each unit of land sold in a discriminating auction can be considered as a separate auction where there are $2m$ combinatorial bidders and n local bidders competing for one unit of land. The expected payoff of the combinatorial bidder j is

(6) $EP_{comb} = E(V | j \text{ wins}) \cdot P(j \text{ wins}) - E(\text{payment}) + B \cdot P(j \text{ wins both objects})$

where $B = (\beta - 1)\, v$ is the net external effect of having both units of land, which is then multiplied with the (joint) probability of winning both units of land (and having a high signal).[163]

The local bidder, on the other hand, has a payoff of

(7) $EP_i = E(V | i \text{ wins}) \cdot P(i \text{ wins}) - E(\text{payment})$

Note that the external effect does not enter the equation. The sum of the expected payoffs of bidders j and i is as follows:

(8) $2m \cdot EP_j + n \cdot EP_i = E(V) - E(\text{Payment}) + 2m \cdot B \cdot P(j \text{ wins 2 objects})$

Thus, the sellers revenue, which is just the expected payment from the two bidders is,

(9) $E(\text{Payment}) = E(V) + 2m \cdot B \cdot P(j \text{ wins 2 objects}) - (2m \cdot EP_{comb} + n \cdot EP_i)$

which is higher when there are no local bidders ($n = 0$).

The implication follows immediately. A policy of having bidders acquire only a single unit of land prevents farmers from realizing external economies, which represents a loss in productive efficiency. This also leads to a lower revenue for the state, reducing the potential gains for the rest of the society in the form of a lower consumer surplus. Thus, although the presence of local bidders is in general welfare reducing, it is much better for the state to encourage such a scheme to be introduced in the auction process.

7.2.3 Multi-stage ascending auction

The problem with a discriminating auction, however, is that the bidders face enormous uncertainty about the strategies of the other bidders. As has been seen, the Nash

---

[163] the assumption on the signals is deleted in the actual modeling. It is assumed that the bidders bid only when they have a highly positive signal on the profitability of the land. In Rosenthal and Wang (1997), this is the case when the bidders receive the signal $S = 1$, which in the end affects the probability estimates of the true value of the good. For the purposes of this analysis, such a detail is not necessary, and saves the effort for the complicated modeling process. Instead, it is just assumed that the bidder has a high estimate of the valuation, which is anyway coming from his signals on the factors that affect the value of the land. See chapter 5 for the details on the affiliation model.

equilibrium strategies of the combinatorial bidders is to bid a value that is less than the mean valuation for the land. This is a result of the inability to collect more information in the process of bidding, particularly on the bids of the others, which in general should reflect the information on their true valuation. In particular, the discriminatory bidding prevents the bidders from raising their bids a bit higher than their individual valuation, simply because if they do, they face the risk of overbidding for a single object if in fact they end up winning only one unit, whereas they could probably do better when they calculate in the external effects of acquiring both units.

The solution to this problem is to allow the bidders to collect information in the process of auctioning. This can be done by adopting a multi-stage auction. As the name suggests, the whole auction procedure is divided into several stages. The privatizing agency announces that the auction will be conducted in, say, a six-month period. At the beginning of the auction, the bidders make an initial offer for the units they are interested in. After each bidding session, the outstanding bids are made public. Thus, the bidders are informed of the latest ranking of the offers, and they can reformulate their strategies according to the current information on the outstanding bids. To the extent that they have made a mistake in their estimation of the value of the land, they would immediately confirm this on the basis of the outstanding bids. They can either adjust their valuations upwards when they have valued the asset too low, or if they valued too high, they can either wait for other re-bidders in the following sessions to raise their bids, or totally pull out in order to avoid the "winner's curse" and minimize their loss.[164] The state can also impose an activity rule, say, an active bidder should bid at least once a month, otherwise, he will be disqualified, and a corresponding penalty is also imposed to guard against having uncommitted bidders.

The combination of having a multi-stage, simultaneous, open ascending auction promotes efficiency. Besides, in the course of the auction, the revenue of the government can only increase but not decrease. A question may be asked as to how the auction will end. A possible solution is to stop the auction when no further bids are tendered on any item[165], because this guards against discriminating any combinatorial bidder with an outstanding bid on say, two items by the very fact of having been able

---

[164] A penalty for withdrawing should be imposed, of course. Otherwise there will be no commitment on the part of the bidders in submitting particular bids. This should be some positive value, at most equal to the difference between the settled price and the bid withdrawn, when the latter is higher.

[165] As in the spectrum auction.

to offer bids that reflect the synergetic effects of having two units. A new bid by another competitor that leaves him with only one unit may suggest overbidding for the one unit left. Such a bidder should again be given a chance to re-bid, or withdraw the other outstanding bid, to minimize loss. This is indeed more efficient.

7.3 Effects of restrictions in land privatization

Some of the restrictions that are commonly imposed in the privatization of land have been discussed earlier. One is the restriction on the qualified bidder for the land. In some cases, the prioritized bidder for the land are the farmers who have been living in the same village for quite some time (as in Germany). In some cases only former land owners who did not get back their lands are given the chance to bid in the sell off. It has been shown that in general, this does not support the efficiency results of an auction. Supporting the formation of combined bids, even to a limited extent, will be welfare-improving.

The other restriction has to do with the moratoria on the resale of the land. This is done to avoid speculative actions on the part of the winning bidders. However, if one has adopted an efficient auction mechanism, there is no reason why this should be a big concern of the state. Firstly, given the current regulations on land use, it will not be easy, if not impossible, to quickly convert agricultural lands into any other non-agricultural use. Therefore, in most cases, the bidders will mainly be those who have a commitment to undertake agricultural production activities. Second, if the auction is conducted widely and as open as possible to everyone who is interested, there will be equal chances for everyone to participate in the sell-off, and further opportunities at gaining economic rent for those who won will be almost nil. The government will have already captured most of the economic rent there is to capture from the bidders, and thus there will be only a few who would take advantage of the resale market just to capture the rent differential. If at all any activity in the secondary market is observed after the auction, this might be due to the effect of uncertainty in the agricultural input as well as output market, which could lead to the phenomenon of the winner's curse. Although the effect of this should have already been minimized in the actual auctioning process, there could still be some cases where an overestimation has occurred. In this case, preventing the farmers from reselling the land that they have acquired will simply worsen the effect of the winner's curse; the ability of the market to correct such miscalculations due to the imperfection of information has been stifled by the policy. This is then counter to the furtherance of the development of the agricultural market, a policy that all of the transforming economies have been campaigning for. Besides, farms who before have a coarser information set will perhaps have a finer information set such that further synergies are discovered; in this case, a well-functioning land market is necessary to promote further increases in efficiency. If the bidders know that there are restrictions on the resale of the land after they have acquired it, then the risk-averse bidder will simply reduce his bid unnecessarily to compensate for the risk of being stuck with a land whose productivity he could have extremely overestimated. On the other hand, it could also be any other reason that has not been anticipated by the bidder during the bidding process. It may be because of a mistake in the estimation of the available funding that he needed to support his agricultural activities, which then makes it difficult for him to undertake the foreseen investment activities that give him his projected income. For the state, intervention in the resale market on the basis of these events will be a waste of the taxpayers' money. In general, the more the state leaves the land market to freely operate like any other land market in established market economies after the completion of privatization, the better it will be for the short as well as the long-term development of the agricultural sector, and the better it will be for the society in general, in terms of keeping the intervention costs at the minimum.

8. Summary and conclusions: Issues and implications in the use of auctions for land privatization

8.1 Economic efficiency and overall welfare effects

It has been shown that land privatization can be treated as a principal-agent problem. The state has the objective of maximizing social welfare in the process of the land ownership transfer, a key activity that needs to be undertaken in the move towards market economy. Given the problems besetting the agricultural land market of the transforming economies, auctions seem to be one of the best mechanisms by which this principal-agent problems can be solved. The privatization program can be implemented such that social welfare of the citizens is maximized. This was shown through the ability of a properly designed auction mechanism to ensure that the resources are allocated to its most efficient use.

Although there are many possible auction institutions that could be considered for privatizing agricultural land in transforming economies, the theory can help to provide guidelines in the design of an efficient mechanism. Even if not all aspects of the reality can be appropriately modeled on very solid theoretical grounds at this point in time, some simple analysis of individual behavior, through the help of game-theoretic models, can show the possible effects of certain institutional regulations on the outcome of the process. This has been the main thrust of the research.

With a simple Bayesian framework, it has been shown that even in the presence of heterogeneity of bidders, efficiency results could still be achieved. Some complicated design mechanisms can be incorporated to treat further complicated cases such as when synergetic effects exist. The analysis has centered mainly on the role of information in the process. The principal-agent problem arises because of the asymmetries in information possessed by the principal and the agent(s). It has been shown that auction mechanisms have the ability to solve the basic problems inherent in the P-A models by making the interested bidders voluntarily reveal their true willingness to pay for the resource. For the privatization of land, the information of interest is the true willingness to pay for the land. But the willingness to pay of the potential farmer-investors is actually only a reflection of how the farmer-bidders have subjectively assessed the maximum potential benefit from the use of the resource would be. Such private information is difficult if not costly for the principal to collect, but its voluntary revelation could be realized given the proper incentives.

Efficiency is shown to be a result that is achieved through the conscious design of the rules and regulations that govern the auction. That is, auctions could possibly lead to conditions worse than merely giving away the resource if some rules have not properly been designed to address the strategic behavior of the bidders. Given this, the main work in the privatization via auctioning of land is rather on the design of the rules of the bidding process. This cannot be emphasized enough, since there have been evidence of governments being too hasty in the design of the process that the rules have been soft on individual strategic behavior, leading to embarrassing outcomes in the privatization process.

This paper has actually focused on the use of a simultaneous, multiple round ascending auction for the sale of agricultural land. The justification rests on the ability of the simultaneous auction to allow the interested bidders to take advantage of the external economies in the use of land as a productive resource in agricultural activities. In essence, such a mechanism incorporates this synergy effects into the competitive bidding process. It has been shown that not only is more efficiency promoted, but that the revenue of the government can even be higher via the adoption of the auction mechanism; a double advantage for the improvement in the welfare of the society.

8.2 Informational burden

One of the reasons for the adoption of an auction mechanism is the lack of information on the part of the privatizing government to set up the appropriate prices of the huge tracks of land that have to be transferred to private hands. There are of course other mechanisms that also ease the informational burden of the government in the privatization process. These are mass privatization and lotteries, among others. It has been shown that such schemes can also be non-discretionary, but no competition has been built into the process. Although the secondary market for the ownership certificates can work properly to establish the right prices, there was no positive inflow of revenue to the government from the privatization process, leading to a condition whereby only the private sector directly involved in the land market would capture the economic rent from the transactions; the potential surplus that could have been created from the revenue of the government has just been transferred to the buyers of land.

The other aspect of importance is the fact that the direct sale via auctioning does not require the government too much effort in monitoring ex post transfer. First of all, it has already captured some of the rent from the buyers of the land – the proceeds of which can be used to provide public goods. Secondly, by the very fact of the efficiency results, there is no clear argument for further use of government funds to make sure that the resource is used optimally. The existing institutional framework that guarantees certain structures to continue to exist, like the restrictions in the outright conversion of agricultural land to non-agricultural uses – will be sufficient for this purposes. This is exactly what differentiates it from the existing system of privatization in the former East Germany. The government has to impose control measures before and after the actual transfer of property rights, because the rules governing the transfer do not guarantee that the good will be given to the individual (juridical or natural) who values it most. The reliance of the process on too much discretion on the part of the bureaucrats has increased the demand for more information that would be too costly to collect for a government machinery that has no direct residual rights on the resource.

8.3 Financial aspects

Transforming economies have always avoided an open announcement of revenue generation as an objective of the privatization process. Given the social and political turmoil that has characterized the process of transformation, it is understandable that this is rather too much political risk to take. However, when one looks at the real issues and the benefits that might come out of an honest desire to improve the welfare of the people, it will be clear that this objective is the most logical of all that provides real welfare increases to the society in general. This is also true in the more advanced Eastern Germany, where the process of land transfer has continued to impose a burden to the government finances too much in the form of administrative costs. The latest debate on this issue focuses on the fact that the German government would have been financially better off to have simply returned the land to the former owners. This is obviously true, but of course it runs counter to the law that has been adopted based on the Two-plus-Four treaty. Such debates have sparked because of the heavy financial distress that the government finds itself in, especially in its bid to push for the

European Monetary Union for which it is one of the main supporters. This in a way puts the German land privatization problem in the same status as that of the other transforming economies; that is, that the financial matters cannot anymore be overlooked. If restitution is not legally possible, then the real alternative is to sell the resource without necessarily compromising the efficiency aspects, because this is vital to the long-term development of the agricultural sector. At the moment, it takes the BVVG at least six months to evaluate a bid for the land, and it has been estimated that, depending on the need for more information, this could extend to two years. This is not only a cost on the part of the government, but also a cost for the bidders, who have to continue to make their financial commitments to their bids binding during the review process. No wonder that there has been little interest in the actual bidding process, such that there are more lands offered now than there are interested bidders. The stakes are much too high for risk averse investors, mainly due to the lack of transparency in the evaluation process. Besides, the current structure of having long-term leases prevents new owners from the immediate use of the resource for what they have foreseen to be the best productive use, again contributing to the additional imputable cost to the acquisition of the land. In the end, these are all foregone earnings for the government; an additional deduction in what would have been a contribution to the society's welfare.

8.4 Equity and fairness

The issues of equity and fairness are important aspects in the design and the implementation of a privatization process. However, this is not to be confused with the social aspects of the transformation problems. Care should be taken that the policy makers in transforming economies do not target a multitude of social objectives in the privatization process that its design and implementation becomes difficult, causing more losses than is necessary. Since land is a highly political resource, many of the privatization programs have suffered due to the attempt of the politicians to address these social problems in the process. Focus must be directed rather on the ability of the privatization program to transfer the resource to private hands in a way that ensures efficiency. But precisely because of this, there is a need to address the issue of designing a program that is equitable and fair. The process should be transparent enough so that the general public may have the chance to check how the rules and regulations are applied. The process should also be non-discretionary, to avoid any individual or particular groups of individuals from being favored, consciously or unconsciously. Addressing both equity and fairness in general prevents or at least minimize rent- seeking activities that lead not only to a waste of resources directly spent on such unproductive activities, but also lead to an inefficient allocation of the state-owned resources.

Apart from the efficiency results of the auction, it shows to be the most fair and equitable of all other methods of privatization that has been used so far in transforming economies. The easy verification of the rules and regulations of the auction make it possible for the general public to evaluate how the privatization is run by the politicians. In other words, it can be made transparent, and thus minimizes corruption.[166] In addition, it does not restrict the resource transfer to a selected few, unlike that in employee privatization schemes.

8.5 Private land market development

The short as well as the long-term development of the agricultural sector rests largely on the ability of the government to commit itself to a truly private-sector-led market by transferring the property rights, legal and physical, to private individuals. Since the market development cannot be undertaken single-handedly by the government, it needs to set up a system that gives incentives to the private sector to invest in the agricultural business enterprises. But this can only be achieved when the government has earned the trust of the private sector via the implementation of a privatization policy that guarantees unrestricted and secure ownership rights to the land. Continued state ownership via privatization methods like leasing stifles the development of the sector, simply because of the lack of a long-term incentive to develop the land and non-land assets towards an optimal size and scope. Auctioning provides a scheme whereby the identified properties are quickly but efficiently transferred to private hands. Further development in the agricultural land market will be based on new information that

---

[166] Russia seems to have realized this lately, and has announced that it will now conduct public auctions of most of its important assets. This has naturally caused rage from those who are used to the old system of insider privatization which has created enormous opportunities for a favored few to accumulate wealth.

comes in about the development of the output and the input markets, which then affects the overall productivity of the farm business. The prospects towards expansion in production and the tapping of new markets abroad will be a task that is more efficiently performed by the private sector. As long as incentives in doing so are present, the private sector will play a key role in the future status of the agricultural sector, specifically in transforming subsistence farms to more commercially-oriented farms. The best that the government can do is to provide the right legal and economic atmosphere for this to be realized.

8.6 Political, institutional, and legal aspects

As has been discussed, the transfer of the ownership of land and non-land assets is a first step towards the long-term development of the agricultural sector. Apart from the requirement that the government must have a strong political will to implement an efficient, equitable and fair privatization process, it must also set up the institutional and legal framework that guarantees that the rights of the new owners of the assets are protected. However, rather than a legal framework that restricts the activities of the new owners of the assets, which is what is now observed in many if not all of the transforming economies, regulations must be designed to help promote private sector investment initiatives. The current restrictions in the land market privatization are inconsistent with the pronouncements of promoting competition and development. Among the legal and institutional set up that have to be considered by the government are: the elimination of moratoria on land sale and controls on sizes, prices and choice of agricultural technology to be used; adoption of an open-information policy on all transactions regarding the privatized land; adoption of a non-discretionary but equitable and fair transfer of property rights that minimizes the cost and maximizes the return to the government in the implementation process; providing an institutional and political framework that allow the new owners to manage the high risk involved the new venture. An example would be to also have a look into innovative rural financia schemes that support the investment in the sector.

In addition, the government must be conscious of its ability to commit to the established policies. A frequently changing policy framework, whether it be macro micro or any other legal and institutional framework increases the uncertainty in the market, which makes the prospective owners more reluctant to venture into the high risk agricultural market. And at the risk of repetition, the government should refrain from using the privatization program as a tool to solve the social problems besetting the agricultural sector, but rather focus on promoting efficiency in the allocation of the resource.

9. Zusammenfassung

Ziel der Arbeit ist es, den Auktionsmechanismus als möglichen Lösungsansatz für das Privatisierungsproblem von Ländern aufzuzeigen, die sich in einem Transformationsprozeß befinden. Dies ist vor allem dann von Bedeutung, wenn es gilt, die Nutzungseffizienz der zu privatisierenden Ressourcen als ein wichtiges Ergebnis zu realisieren.

Die Analyse des Bodenmarktes wurde deshalb als Beispiel gewählt, weil u.a. die Privatisierung von staatlichem Eigentum an Grund und Boden eines der Verfahren ist, deren Gestaltung besonders kompliziert und problematisch ist. Gründe hierfür sind z.B. die emotionale Bindung des Volkes an das Land und die vielseitigen Nutzungsmöglichkeiten des Bodens als eine produktive Ressource.

Kern der Analyse ist die Anwendung eines informationstheoretischen Ansatzes in Form Bayes'scher Modellierungsprozesse, insbesondere jedoch die Theorie der Mechanismusges-taltung was einer Ausweitung des üblichen neoklassischen Ansatzes gleichkommt.

Es soll gezeigt werden, daß das Privatisierungsproblem im Bodenmarkt grundsätzlich als Prinzipal-Agent (PA)-Problem dargestellt werden kann. Der Staat agiert hierbei als Prinzipal, und die Interessenten übernehmen die Rolle der Agenten. Das Ziel des Staates, nämlich die Maximierung der sozialen Wohlfahrt, könnte durch einen ordentlich gestalteten Auktionsmechanismus realisiert werden mit einer effizienten Ressourcennutzung als direktes Ergebnis des Bietprozesses. Eine Auktion könnte also das PA-Problem der Privatisierung lösen, indem sie den freien Zugang zu privaten asymmetrischen Informationen, die Verursacher des PA-Problems, für den Prinzipal der Auktion ermöglicht.

Es wurde gezeigt, daß insbesondere ein sich in simultanen multiplen Runden steigernder Bietprozeß ein idealer Mechanismus ist, um die Besonderheiten des Bodenmarktes miteinzubeziehen. Durch die damit einhergehende Maximierung des Veräußerungserlöses läßt sich die Steigerung der sozialen Wohlfahrt, die der Staat mit der Veräußerung seines Eigentums an Grund und Boden erreichen will, noch steigern. Wie bereits im vorherigen Absatz erwähnt wurde, ist die Durchführung einer Privatisierung wegen der asymmetrischen Informationsverteilung zwischen Staat und

Interessenten problematisch, wenn die Vergabe im Hinblick auf die Erreichung der größtmöglichen Effizienz erfolgen soll. Neben dem Auktionsmechanismus gibt es andere Privatisierungsmethoden, durch die die Zuteilung privater asymmetrischer Informationen realisiert werden kann. Ihr Nachteil ist jedoch, daß sie den Wettbewerb normalerweise nicht miteinbeziehen.

Auch wenn diese Privatisierungsmethoden gegenüber dem Auktionsmechanismus nicht grundsätzlich diskriminierend betrachtet werden sollten, so muß doch festgehalten werden, daß sie die Effizienz eines Ergebnisses nicht garantieren können. Der Grund hierfür liegt u.a. in der Existenz eines Moral Hazard Problems, das erst nach der Privatisierung, also ex post, offensichtlich wird. Zusätzliche Maßnahmen könnten die Effizienz der durch diese Methoden erreichten Ergebnisse steigern, doch sind sie meistens mit erheblichen Kosten für die Regierung, so z.B. durch die Notwendigkeit weiterer Informationsbeschaffung oder Monitoring ex post, verbunden. Bei manchen Privatisierungsmethoden spielt der sekundäre Markt eine wichtige Rolle, um die Preise zu korrigieren. In diesem Fall ist die Effizienz gewährleistet. Das Problem ist, daß die Maximierung des Veräußerungserlöses mit Absicht nicht erzielt wurde, ein Vorgang, der in der ehemaligen DDR zu beobachten ist. Ein Transfer der ökonomischen Rente findet in diesen Fällen nur zwischen der Regierung und den Käufern statt. Die restliche Bevölkerung hat keinen Nutzen von der Privatisierung bzw. dem Transfer der ökonomischen Rente des Bodens. Die Auktion ist daher ein besserer Mechanismus, da sie keinen weiteren Informationsbedarf benötigt, um die Effizienz der Ergebnisse zu sichern. Durch die Erlöse könnten zusätzlich öffentliche Güter geliefert werden.

Gerechtigkeit ist ein wichtiger Aspekt der Privatisierung. Dennoch sollte man die Gerechtigkeit, die durch die Implementierung eines Privatisierungsprogramms mitein-bezogen werden soll, nicht mit der sozialen und wirtschaftliche Gerechtigkei verwechseln, die im Rahmen des Transformationsprozesses zu realisieren wünscht. Ir den meisten Fällen haben Politiker versucht, die sozialen und wirtschaftlicher Probleme, die während des Transformationsprozesses auftraten, durch Privatisierunger zu lösen. Soziale bzw. Gerechtigkeitsprobleme können jedoch nur durch eine sinnvolle Sozialpolitik und nicht durch die Implementierung eines Privatisierungsprogramm: gelöst werden. Eine Politisierung des Privatisierungsprogrammes führt zu zusätzlicher und meist unerwarteten Problemen, ohne daß das eigentliche Ziel der Privatisierung erreicht wird. In einem Auktionsmechanismus wird die Gerechtigkeit hingegen ir Form von leicht verifizierbaren Implementierungsregelungen von Anfang ar

Sappington, D.E.M. and J. Stiglitz (1987). Privatization, Information, and Incentives. *Journal of Policy Analysis and Management.* 6 (4) pp. 567-82.

Savoie, D. J. and I. Brecher (1992). *Equity and Efficiency in Economic Development: Essays in Honour of Benjamin Higgins.* McGill-Queen's University Press.

Schleifer A. (1995). Establishing Property Rights. In *WB Proceedings of the 1994 Annual Conference on Development Economics.* IBRD.

Schleifer A. and R. Vishny (1994). Politicians and Firms. *Quarterly Journal of Economics.* 109: pp. 995-1025.

Schönberg, O.F.(1997). Pachten statt Kaufen. *DLG Mitteilungen.* 5 p. 32.

Sengupta, J.(1993). *Econometrics of Information and Efficiency.* The Netherlands: Kluwer Academic Publishers.

Shapiro, C. and J. Stiglitz (1984). Equilibrium Unemployment as a Discipline Device. *American Economic Review.* 74: pp. 433-444.

Shapiro C. and R.D. Willig. Economic Rationales for the Scope of Privatization. In Suleimann E.N. and J. Waterbury. *The Political Economy of Public Sector Reform and Privatization.* Oxford: Westview Press. pp. 57-87.

Siebert, H. (1993) The Big Bang with the Big Brother: German Reunification in its Third Year. Kiel Discussion Papers No. 211. Institut für Weltwirtschaft Kiel.

Siebert, H.,ed. (1992) *Privatization.* Symposium in Honour of Herbert Giersch. Tübingen: J.C. B. Mohr

Sinn, G. and H.W. Sinn (1992). *Jumpstart.* Economic Unification of Germany. Massachussets: MIT Press.

Smith, V., ed. (1985). *Research in Experimental Economics.* Vol. 3 Greenwich, CT, JAI Press.

Smith, V. (1989) Theory, Experiment and Economics. *Journal of Economic Perspectives.* 3 (1): pp. 151-169.

Spence, A.M. (1973). Job Market Signalling. *Quarterly Journal of Economics.* 87: pp. 355-374.

Stiglitz, J.E. (1993). Incentives, Organizational Structures, and Contractual Choice in the Reform of Socialist Agriculture. In Braverman, A., K-M. Brooks, C. Csaki (eds). *The Agricultural Transition in Central and Eastern Europe and the Former USSR.* The World Bank; Washington DC. pp. 27-46.

miteinbezogen. Dies verhindert die Verschwendung von Ressourcen durch ökonomisch unproduktive Aktivitäten wie z.B. Korruption.

Die lang- bzw. kurzfristige Entwicklung eines funktionierenden Bodenmarktes liegt in der Förderung der Aktivitäten des privaten Sektors. Dabei ist es erforderlich, Möglichkeiten für einen ernsthaften Transfer des Property Rights an private Unternehmen, Institutionen und Individuen zu schaffen. Dies ist ein fundamentaler Schritt auf dem Weg zu einer erfolgreichen Transformation. Die Regierung wird bei gleichen Kosten nie in der Lage sein, sich bessere Informationen als die privaten Individuen anzueignen. Es ist besser, den Markt und seine auf ihm stattfindenden Aktivitäten allein den richtigen Entwicklungspfad finden zu lassen. Wenn ein Monitoring nach der Privatisierung benötigt wird, um die Effizienz der privatisierten Güter zu sichern, ist ein erheblicher Informationsaufwand von Seiten der Regierung notwendig. Ein physikalischer als auch rechtlicher Transfer des Property Rights durch eine Auktion schafft nicht nur kurzfristige Effizienz durch die schnelle Vergabe des Gutes an den Meistbietenden, sondern auch langfristige Effizienz durch die Schaffung von Anreizen für ihre neuen privaten Besitzer, neue Informationen zu bekommen, um die Ressourcennutzung stetig zu verbessern und Gewinne zu maximieren.

Die Regierung spielt bei diesem Vorgang eine wichtige Rolle, denn sie muß die für den Erfolg der Markt- bzw. Wirtschaftsentwicklung notwendigen Rahmenbedingungen bereitstellen. Das heißt, sie muß ein institutionelles und rechtliches System schaffen, das die Besitz- und Rechtsansprüche der neuen Besitzer gewährleistet. Es muß betont werden, es für den Agrarmarkt in transformierenden Länder immer schwieriger wird, einer Entwicklung zu folgen, die durch die zunehmende Anzahl von Restriktionen auf dem Bodenmarkt bestimmt wird. Eine Regierung kann ihr Versprechen, ihr Land durch einen bedeutsamen Transformationsprozeß zu führen, am besten glaubhaft machen, indem sie sich zu einer beständigen langfristig ausgelegten Politik verpflichtet und diese auch mit möglichst wenig Interventionen beibehält.

10. References

Agrarbericht 1995, 1996.

Agrarsoziale Gesellschaft (ed., 1994) *Die Zukunft der landwirtschaftlichen Flächen: Nutzungen, Wertungen, Prognosen.* Göttingen: Agrarsoziale Gesellschaft, e.V.

Arrow, K. (1951) *Social Choice and Individual Values.* New York: Wiley.

Akerlof, G. (1970). The Market for Lemons. Quality Uncertainty and the Market Mechanism. *Quarterly Journal of Economics*, 89 (3)August, pp. 488-500.

Andreff, W. (1992). French privatization techniques and experience: a model for Central-Eastern Europe? in Targetti, Ferdinando. *Privatization in Europe: West and East Experiences.* Darthmouth Publishing.

Aoki, M. und H-K. Kim (1995). Unternehmensführung in den Transformationsländern. *Finanzierung und Entwicklung.* IMF and WB. September issue.

Arrow K. and L. Hurwicz (1977). *Studies in Resource Allocation Processes.* Cambridge University Press.

Bazermann M. and W. Samuelson (1983). The Winner's Curse: An Empirical Investigation. in R. Tietz, ed. *Aspiraton Levels in Bargaining and Economic Decision-Making.* New York: Springer-verlag. pp. 186-200.

Bazermann M. and W. Samuelson. (1983). I Won the Auction, but I don't Want the Prize. *Journal of Conflict Resolution*, 27, December: pp. 618-34.

Bester, H. (1985). Screening vs. Rationing in Credit Markets with Imperfect Information. *American Economic Review.* 75 (4) pp. 850-855.

Bishop, M. R., and J. Kay. (1991) "Privatization in Western Economies." in Siebert, Horst, ed. *Privatization.* Kiel: Institut für Weltwirtschaft. pp. 193-209

Boardman A.E. and A.R. Vining (1989). Ownership and Performance in Competitive Environments: A Comparison of the Performance of Private, Mixed, and State-Owned Enterprises. *Journal of Law and Economics.* 32: pp. 1-33.

Böhme, K. (1996). Zum Verfahren für den begünstigten Bodenerwerb durch Pächter. *Neue Landwirtschaft - Briefe zum Agrarrecht.* 8: pp. 186-194.

Borcheling, T.E., W.W. Pommerenhe and F. Schneider (1982). Comparing the Efficiency of Private and Public Production: The Evidence from Five Countries. In Bös, D., R.A. Musgrave and J. Wiseman, eds. *Public Production*. Vienna, Springer. (Zeitschrift für National Ökonomie/Journal of Economics, Supplement 2)

Bös, D. (1991). *Privatization: A Theoretical Treatment*. Oxford University Press.

Boycko, M, A. Schleifer, R. W. Vishny.(1996). A Theory of Privatization. *The Economic Journal*. 106 (March): pp. 309-319.

Brada, J. (1996) Privatization is Transition - Or Is It? *Journal of Economic Perspectives* 10 (2): pp. 67-86.

Braun, J. and H.P. Weikard (1994) Auction Models of Privatization of Agricultural Land in Eastern Germany. Universität Göttingen, Institut für Agrarökonomie: Diskussionsbeitrag 9406.

Braverman, A., K-M. Brooks, C. Csaki , eds. (1993). *The Agricultural Transition in Central and Eastern Europe and the Former USSR*. The World Bank; Washington DC.

Brooks K., (1993). Property Rights in Land. in Braverman, A., K-M. Brooks, C. Csaki, eds. *The Agricultural Transition in Central and Eastern Europe and the Former USSR*. The World Bank; Washington DC. pp. 125-136.

Bulow, J. and P. Klemperer. Auctions versus Negotiations.(1996) *American Economic Review*. March issue. 86 (7): pp. 180-194.

Bulow, J. and J. Roberts (1989) The Simple Economics of Optimal Auctions. *Journal of Political Economy*. 97 (5): pp. 1060-1090.

BVVG. *Fragen und Antworten zum Flächenerwerb nach dem Entschädigungs- und Ausgleichsleistungsgesetz in den fünf neuen Bundesländern.*

Che, Y. K.(1993) Design Competition through Multidimensional Auctions. *RAND Journal of Economics* 24: pp. 669-680.

Chilosi, A. (1995). Privatization in Eastern European Transition: Economic Consequences of Alternative Privatization Processes. In Daviddi R. ed. *Property Rights and Privatization in the Transition to Market Economy: A Comparative Review*. European Institute of Public Administration. Netherlands. pp.63-101.

Chipman, J.S., D. McFadden, and M.K. Richter, eds.(1990) *Preferences, Uncertainty and Optimality. Essays in Honor of Leonid Hurwicz*. Westview Press.

162

Chung, K.L. (1979). *Elementary Probability Theory with Stochastic Processes.* Springer-Verlag.

Clarke, T. (1994). Introduction: Privatizing the World? In Clarke, T., ed. *International Privatization: Strategies and Practices.* Walter de Gruyter. Berlin. pp. 1-22.

Clarke, T., ed. (1994). *International Privatization: Strategies and Practices.* Walter de Gruyter. Berlin.

Coase, R. (1960). The Problem of Social Cost. *Journal of Law and Economics.* 3: pp. 1-44.

Csaki C. and Z. Lerman (1994). Land Reform and Farm Sector Restructuring in the Former Socialist Countries of Europe. *European Review of Agricultural Economics.* 21: pp. 553-576.

Csaki, C. and Z. Lerman (1996). Agricultural Transition Revisited: Issues of Land Reform and Farm Restructuring in East Central Europe and the Former USSR. *Quarterly Journal of International Agriculture.* 25 (3): pp. 211-240.

Daviddi, R. (1995). Privatization in the Transition to a Market Economy. in Daviddi, R.,ed. (1995). *Property Rights and Privatization in the Transition to Market Economy: A Comparative Review.* European Institute of Public Administration. Netherlands. pp. 1-30.

Daviddi, R.,ed. (1995). *Property Rights and Privatization in the Transition to Market Economy: A Comparative Review.* European Institute of Public Administration. Netherlands.

Doll, H., H.-J. Günther und K. Klare (1994). Empirische Analyse der Pachtmärkte in Mecklenburg-Vorpommern. Lanbauforschung Völkenrode 44 (1)   pp. 54-66.

Doll, H., H.-J. Günther, K. Hagedorn, B. Klages, K. Klare (1994). *Untersuchung der Privatisierung volkseigener landwirtschaftlicher Flächen durch die Treuhandanstalt (THA) - Zwischenbericht.* Braunschweig: Institut für Strukturforschung der Bundesanstalt für Landwirtschaft (FAL).

Eatwell, J., et.al, eds., *The New Palgrave: Allocation, Information and Markets.* Basingstoke: McMillan.

Economic Commission for Europe (1995). *Economic Survey of Europe in 1994-95.* United Nations.

Engelbrecht-Wiggans, R. (1980). Auctions and Bidding Models: A Survey. *Management Science* 26 (2): pp. 119-142.

Englebrecht.Wiggans, R., M. Schubik and R.M. Staub. (1983). *Auctions, Bidding and Contracting: Uses and Theory*. New York University Press.

Federal Communications Commission (FCC) (1993). *Fifth Report and Order*. PC Docket No. 93-253. Washington, D.C.

Federal Communications Commission (FCC) (1993). *Second Report and Order*. PP Docket No. 93-253. Washington, D.C.

Feltham, G.A., A. H. Amershi and W. T. Ziemba (1988*). Economic Analysis of Information and Contracts*. Essays in Honor of John E. Butterworth. Boston: Kluwer Academic Publishers.

Fudenberg, D. and J. Tirole.(1991) *Game Theory*. Cambridge, MIT.

Funke, N. (1993). The Design and Sequencing of Reforms: Competing Views and the Role of Credibility. *Kyklos*. 46: pp. 337-362.

Garvin, S. and J. H. Kagel (1994). Learning in Common Value Auctions: Some Initial Observations. *Journal of Economic Behaviour and Organization*. 25: pp. 351-372.

Gesetz zur Privatisierung und Reorganisation des volkseigenen Vermögens (Treuhandgesetz) vom 17. Juni 1990.

Ghaussy, A. Ghanie and Wolf Schäfer, eds. (1993). *The Economics of German Unification*. London: Routledge.

Gibbard, A. (1973). Manipulation of Voting Schemes. *Econometrica* 41: pp. 587-601.

Gibbons, R. (1992). *Game Theory for Applied Economists*. Princeton University Press.

Gray, C.W. (1996). In Search of Owners: Privatization and Corporate Governance in Transition Economies. *The World Bank Research Observer*, 11 (2): pp. 179-197.

Grossman S.J. and O:D. Hart (1983). An Analysis of the Principal-Agent Problem. *Econometrica* 51: pp. 7-45.

Groves, T. R. Radner and S. Reiter, eds.(1987). *Information, Incentives, and Economic Mechanisms: Essays in Honor of Leonid Hurwicz*. Basil Blackwell Ltd.

Hagedorn K. und Klages B. (1994). *Konzepte zur Privatisierung volkseigenen landwirtschaftlichen Bodens und Entwürfe zum Entschädigungs- und Ausgleichsleistungsgesetz: Analyse und Alternativen*. Landbauforschung Völkenrode 44 (1): pp. 44-53.

Hansen R. G. and J.R. Lott. (1991). The Winner's Curse and Public Information in Common Value Auctions: Comment. *American Economic Review*. 81 (1): pp. 347-361.

Hausch, D. (1986). Multi-object Auctions: Sequential vs. Simultaneous Sales. *Management Science*. 32 (12): pp. 1599-1610.

Hax, H. (1991). Privatization Agencies: The Treuhand Approach. in: Siebert, H., ed. *Privatization*. Tubingen: Mohr.

Hayek, F. A. (1945). The Use of Knowledge in Society. *American Economic Review*. 35 (4) Sept.: pp. 519-530.

Henderson, J. and R. Quandt (1980). *Microeconomic Theory: A Mathematical Approach*. McGraw Hill.

Hendricks, K. and R. Porter. (1980). An Empirical Study of an Auction with Asymmetric Information. *Operations Research*. pp. 865-903.

Henning, F. W. (1978). *Landwirtschaft und ländliche Gesellschaft in Deutschland*. Band 2. pp. 1750-1976. Paderborn: Schöningh.

Heuer, K. (1991). *Grundzüge des Bodenrechts der DDR 1949-1989*. München: C.H. Beck.

Higgins, B. (1992). Equity and Efficiency in Development: Basic Concepts. in Savoie, D. J. and I. Brecher. *Equity and Efficiency in Economic Development: Essays in Honour of Benjamin Higgins*. McGill-Queen's University Press.

Holt, C.H. (1980). Competitive Bidding for Contracts under Alternative Auction Procedures. *Journal of Political Economy*. 88 (31): pp 433-445

Höper, H. (1985). *Die Bestimmungsfaktoren des Bodenpreises, die Bodenpreisbildung und die Auswirkungen staatlicher Eingriffe, gem. Grundstücksverkehrsgesetz auf den Bodenmarkt*. Kiel: Vauk.

Hurwicz L. (1977). On the Dimensional Requirements of Informationally-decentralized Pareto-satisfactory Processes. In Arrow, K.J. and L. Hurwicz, eds. *Studies in Resource Allocation Processes*. Cambridge University Press. pp. 413-424.

Hurwicz, L. (1972). On Informationally Decentralized Systems. in: McGuire, C.B./ Radner, R. eds., *Decision and Organization*. A Volume in Honor of Jacob Marschak. Amsterdam: North-Holland. pp. 297-336.

Immler, H. (1971). *Agrarpolitik in der DDR*. Köln: Verlag Wissenschaft und Politik.

Inotai, A. (1992). Experience with Privatization in East Central Europe. in: Siebert, H., ed. *Privatization*. Tübingen: Mohr. pp. 163-182.

Kagel, J.H. and Levin, D. (1986). The Winner's Curse and Public Information in Common Value Auctions. *American Economic Review*. 6 (5): pp. 894-920.

Kreps, D. M.(1990). *A Course in Microeconomic Theory*. Simon and Schuster.

Krishna, V. And R.W. Rosenthal.(1996). Simultaneous Auctions with Synergies. *Games and Economic Behavior* 17: pp. 1-31.

Laffont, J.J. and J. Tirole (1994). *A Theory of Incentives in Procurement and Regulation.* MIT.

Ledyard, J. O. (1989). "Incentive Compatibility" in Eatwell, John, et. al, eds., *The New Palgrave: Allocation, Information and Markets.* Basingstoke: McMillan. pp. 739-743.

Levin, J. (1997) An Optimal Auction for Complements. *Games and Economic Behavior.* 18: pp. 176-192.

Levin, D., J. H. Kagel and J.F. Richard. (1996) Revenue Effects and Information Processing in English and Common Value Auctions. *IFO Studien.* (1). pp. 442-460.

Lind, B. and C.H. Plott (1991). The Winner's Curse: Experiments with Buyers and Sellers. *American Economic Review.* 81 (1): pp. 335-346.

Madden, B.J. and L.R. Malcolm (1996). Deciding on the Worth of Agricultural Land. *Review of Marketing and Agricultural Economics.* 64 (2): pp. 152-165.

Maskin, E. (1992). Auctions in Privatization. In Siebert, H.,ed. *Privatization. Symposium in Honour of Herbert Giersch.* Tübingen: J.C. B. Mohr. pp. 115-36.

McAfee, R. P. and J. McMillan (1987). Auctions and Bidding. *Journal of Economic Literature* 25: pp. 699-738.

McAfee, R.P. und J. McMillan (1996). Analyzing the Airwaves Auction. *Journal of Economic Perspectives.* 10 (1): pp. 159-175.

McAfee R.P. and D. Vincent (1997). Sequentially Optimal Auctions. Games and Economic Behavior. 18: pp. 246-276.

McMillan, J. (1994). The Sale of Spectrum Rights. *Journal of Economic Perspectives.* 8 (3): pp. 145-162.

Merkel, K. and E. Schuhans (1960). *Die Agrarwirtschaft in Mitteldeutschland.* Bonn: Deutscher Bundes-Verlag.

Milgrom P. and R. Weber (1982). A Theory of Auctions and Competitive Bidding. *Econometrica.* 50 (5): pp. 1089-1122.

Milgrom, P. (1979). A Convergence Theorem for Competitive Bidding with Differential Information. *Econometrica.* 47 (3): pp. 679- 688.

Milgrom, P. (1981). Rational Expectations, Information Acquisition, and Competitive Bidding. *Econometrica*. July issue. 49 (4): pp. 921-943.

Milgrom, P. (1981). An Axiomatic Characterization of Common Knowledge. *Econometrica*. 49 (1): pp. 219-222.

Milgrom, P. (1983). Private Information in an Auctionlike Securities Market. In Engelbrecht-Wiggans, K. *Auctions, Bidding and Contracting: Uses and Theory*. New York University Press. pp. 137-148.

Milgrom, P. (1989). Auctions and Bidding: A Primer. *Journal of Economic Perspectives*. 3 (3): pp. 3-22.

Milgrom, P. (1998). *Auctions in Privatization*. Cambridge University Press.

Milgrom, P. and J. Roberts (1992). *Economics, Organization, and Management*. New Jersey: Prentice-Hall.

Miller, P. J. (1994). *The Rational Expectations Revolutions*. MIT Press.

Milward R. And D.M. Parker (1983). Public and Private Enterprise: Comparative Behaviour and Relative Efficiency. In Milward, R. D.M Parker, L. Rosenthal M.T. Summer and T. Topham, eds (1983) *Public Sector Economics*. London; Longman.

Milward, R. D.M Parker, L. Rosenthal M.T. Summer and T. Topham, eds (1983*) Public Sector Economics. London*; Longman.

Murrell P. (1991). Can Neoclassical Economics Underpin the Reform of Centrally Planned Economies? *Journal of Economic Perspectives*. 5 (4): pp. 59-76.

Myerson, R. (1981). Optimal Auction Design. *Mathematics of Operations Research*. 6 (1): pp. 58-75.

Myerson R.B. and M.A. Satterthwaite (1983). Efficient Mechanisms for Bilateral Trading. *Journal of Economic Theory* 28: pp. 265-81.

Myerson, R. (1989). Mechanism Design. in Eatwell, J., et.al, eds., *The New Palgrave: Allocation, Information and Markets*. Basingstoke: McMillan. pp. 191-206.

Neubäumer, R. (1996). Erfolge und Probleme im deutschen Vereinigungsprozeß. *Wirtschaftsdienst*. 9: pp. 574-591.

OECD (1993). *Transformation of the Banking System: Portfolio Restructuring, Privatization and the Payment System*.

Paque, K.H., et al. (1993) Challenges Ahead: Long-term Perspectives of the German Economy. Kiel Discussion Papers No. 202/203. Kiel: Institut für Weltwirtschaft.

Prokopenko, J., ed. (1995). *Management for Privatization: Lessons from Industry and Public Service*. International Labour Organization.

Rapaczynski, A. (1996). The Roles of the State and the Market in Establishing Property Rights. *Journal of Economic Perspectives*. 10 (2): pp. 87-103.

Rasmusen E.(1994). *Games and Information*. Second edition. Blackwell Publishers, Inc.

Reiter, S. (1989). Efficient Allocation. in Eatwell, John, Murray Milgate and Peter Newman, eds. *The New Palgrave: Allocation, Information and Markets*. The Macmillan Press Limited, London.

Richtlinie für die Durchführung der Verwertung und Verwaltung volkseigener land- und forstwirtschaftlicher Flächen vom 26.6.1992 in der Fassung vom 22.6.1993.

Riley J.G. (1988). Ex-Post Information in Auctions. *Review of Economic Studies*. 40: pp. 409-30.

Riley, J.G. and W.F. Samuelson. (1981). Optimal Auctions. *American Economic Review*. 71: pp. 381-392.

Rondinelli, D.A. (1995). Privatization and Economic Transformation: The Management Challenge. In Prokopenko, J., ed. *Management for Privatization: Lessons from Industry and Public Service*. International Labour Organization. pp. 3-45.

Rosenthal. R. and R. Wang (1996). Simultaneous Auctions with Synergies and Common Values. *Games and Economic Behaviour*. 17: pp. 32-55.

Roth, A. and J.K Murnighan (1982). The Role of Information in Bargaining: An Experimental Study. *Econometrica* 50 (5): pp. 1123- 1141.

Rothkopf, M.H. (1980). On Multiplicative Bidding Strategies. *Operations Research*. pp. 570-575.

Samuelson W.F. and Bazerman, M.H. (1985). The Winners Curse in Bilateral Negotiations. In Smith, V.L. ed. *Research in Experimental Economics*. Greenwich, CT, JAI Press. 3: pp. 105-137.

Samuelson, P. (1990). Stochastic Land Valuation: Total Returns as Martingale Implying Price Changes a Negatively Correlated Random Walk. in Chipman, J.S., D. McFadden, and M.K. Richter, eds. *Preferences, Uncertainty and Optimality. Essays in Honor of Leonid Hurwicz*. Westview Press. pp. 241-253.

Sappington, D. E. M (1991). Incentives in Principal-agent Relationships. *Journal of Economic Perspectives*. 5 (2): pp.45-66.

Suleimann E.N. and J. Waterbury. *The Political Economy of Public Sector Reform and Privatization*. Oxford: Westview Press

Takayama, A. (1985) *Mathematical Economics*. Second Edition. Cambridge University Press.

Targetti, F. (1992). Privatization in Europe: West and East Experiences. Darthmouth Publishing.

Targetti, F. (1992) The Privatization Of Industry With Particular Regard To Economies In Transition. in F. Targetti, ed.. *Privatization in Europe: West and East Experiences*. Dartmouth Publishing Co, England.

Thaler, R. (1992).*The Winner's Curse: Paradoxes and Anomalies of the Everyday Economic Life*. Maxwell Macmillan Canada.

Thiel, S.T. (1988). Some Evidence of the Winner's curse. *American Economic Review*. pp. 884-895.

Thiemeyer, T. (1986). Privatization: On the many senses in which this word is used in international discussion on Economic Theory. in T. Thiemeyer and G. Quaden, eds. *The Privatization of Public Enterprises: A European Debate*. Liège: CIRIEC (Annals of Public and Cooperative Economy), Special Issue.

Varian, H. (1992) *Microeconomic Analysis*. Third Edition. W.W. Norton Company.

Vernon R. (1988). Introduction: The Promise and Challenge. In Vernon, R. (ed). *The Promise of Privatization*. New York, Council of Foreign Relations. pp. 1-22.

Vickers, J. and G. Yarrow (1991). Economic Perspectives on Privatization. *Journal of Economic Perspectives*. 5 (4): pp. 111 - 132.

Vickrey, W. (1961). Counterspeculation, Auctions and Competitive Sealed Tenders. *Journal of Finance* 16 (1): pp. 8-37

Vickrey W. (1962). Auctions and Bidding Games. *Recent Advances in Game Theory*. Princeton University Press. pp. 15-27.

Waldron, J. (1988) *The Right to Private Property*. Oxford: Clarendon Press.

Weber R. (1983). Multiple-Object Auctions. In Englebrecht.Wiggans, R., M. Schubik and R.M. Staub. *Auctions, Bidding and Contracting: Uses and Theory*. New York University Press. pp. 165-191.

Wilson, R. (1992). Strategic Analysis of Auctions. *Handbook on Game Theory*. Elsevier Science Publishers, B.V. pp. 227-279.

Winkler, R. L. and D.G. Brooks (1980). Competitive Bidding with Dependent Value Estimate. *Operations Research*. May-June. pp. 603-613.

World Bank (1994) *Annual Conference on Development Economics*. Washington D.C.

Xu, F. R. C. Mittelhammer, and P. W. Barkley (1993). Measuring the Contributions of Site Characteristics to the Value of Agricultural Land. *Land Economics*. 69 (4): pp. 356-369.

DUV Deutscher UniversitätsVerlag
GABLER·VIEWEG·WESTDEUTSCHER VERLAG

"Kasseler Wirtschafts- und Verwaltungswissenschaften"

Herausgeber: Prof. Dr. Heinz Hübner, Prof. Dr. Jürgen Reese,
Prof. Dr. Peter Weise, Prof. Dr. Udo Winand
GABLER EDITION WISSENSCHAFT

Band 1: Heinz Hübner/Torsten Dunkel (eds.),
Recent Essentials in Innovation Management and Research
Networking, Innovation Systems, Instruments, Ecology
in International Perspective
1995. ISBN 3-8244-6253-2

Band 2: Karsten Schweichhart,
Modellierung persönlichen und privaten Wissens
Individuelle Systeme zur Datenrecherche und Vortragserstellung
1996. ISBN 3-8244-6318-0

Band 3: Christian Zich, **Integrierte Typen- und Teileoptimierung**
Neue Methoden des Produktprogramm-Managements
1996. ISBN 3-8244-6338-5

Band 4: Hermann-Josef Kiel, **Dienstleistungen und Regionalentwicklung**
Ansätze einer dienstleistungsorientierten Strukturpolitik
1996. ISBN 3-8244-6438-1

Band 5: Karsten Tiemann, **Investor Relations**
Bedeutung für neu am Kapitalmarkt eingeführte Publikumsgesellschaften
1997. ISBN 3-8244-6461-6

Band 6: Monika Vogt, **Tourenplanung in Ballungsgebieten**
Entwicklung eines PC-gestützten Verfahrens
1998. ISBN 3-8244-6730-5

Band 7: Jocelyn Braun, **Large-scale Privatisation via Auctions**
The case of land in transforming economies
1998. ISBN 3-8244-6777-1

Band 8: Martina Schulze, **Nachfragemacht im Lebensmitteleinzelhandel**
Ökonomische und kartellrechtliche Aspekte
1998. ISBN 3-8244-6770-4

Deutscher Universitäts-Verlag
Postfach 30 09 44
51338 Leverkusen